LAMDA
ANTHOLOGY OF VERSE AND PROSE

LAMDA

ANTHOLOGY OF VERSE AND PROSE

VOLUME XIV

Introduction by Timothy West, CBE, FRSA

PUBLISHED BY
OBERON BOOKS
FOR THE LONDON ACADEMY OF MUSIC AND
DRAMATIC ART

ACKNOWLEDGEMENTS

For permission to reprint the copyright material in this anthology we make grateful acknowledgement to the following authors, publishers and executors:

Bloodaxe Books for A Student Drama Group Performs In An Old Peoples' Home by John Cassidy from Night Cries by John Cassidy (Bloodaxe Books 1982); Brimax for Two Witches by Alexander Resnikoff; Julius Chingono for The Sun; James Clarke & Co, The Lutterworth Press for Hide And Seek and The Man Outside from Whispers From A Wardrobe by Richard Edwards; John Coldwell for Snow Problem; Curtis Brown Ltd London for Cold Comfort Farm by Stella Gibbons; The Estate of Roy Fuller for Translation by Roy Fuller; Faber & Faber Ltd for Boy At The Window by Richard Wilbur from New and Collected Poems, Moondial by Helen Cresswell, The Mouse and His Child by Russell Hoban; Film Rights Ltd in association with Laurence Fitch for I Capture The Castle by Dodie Smith; Grolier Publishing for Chocolates by Louis Simpson; Harper Collins Publishers Ltd for Dormouse and Caravans by Lillian McCrea, Jumping Rhyme by Anne English, Open Windows by Alexander Franklin, Song of the Washing Machine by Donald Mattam, The Moon of Gomrath by Alan Garner, The Leopard by Giuseppe de Lampedusa (published by Collins Harvill, an imprint of HarperCollins Publishers Ltd); David Higham Associates for Titus Groan by Mervyn Peake (published by Penguin), Green Man Blue Man by Charles Causely from Figgie Hobbin (published by Macmillan), The Incredible Journey by Sheila Burnford (published by Hodder & Stoughton), Brighton Rock by Graham Greene (published by Heinemann),The Towers of Silence by Paul Scott (published by Penguin); Hodder & Stoughton Ltd for Children on the Oregon Trail by A Rutgers van der Loeff, The Lake at the End of the World by Caroline MacDonald; David Jackson for Where's Your Homework, reprinted by kind permission of the author; John Kitching for It's Not My Fault, reprinted by kind permission of the author; Edite Kroll Literary Agency for It's Dark In Here by Shel Silverstein from Where The Sidewalk Ends copyright 1974 by Evil Eye Music Inc; Larousse plc for The Story of King Arthur by Robin Lister, copyright Grisewood

CONTENTS

INTRODUCTION

We live, we are told, in an age of visual images. Fewer and fewer people in this country, apparently, are learning to read properly: language has become subservient to pictures. This is the received wisdom that informs the TV and film industry today... and yet how many times are they proved wrong? So often it's the well-turned verbal joke that gets the laugh, the spoken word that moves or shocks, the line of dialogue that we remember when the pictorial image is forgotten.

It is hard to reconcile the gloomy forebodings about falling standards of literacy with the fact that - for instance - more poetry is written, published, spoken publicly, and presumably read, in this country than ever before. Plays, old and new, that celebrate the use of language are produced regularly and successfully, and a national organisation is pledged to the continuous presentation of Shakespeare. Two-volume novels are now listened to on tape, driving up the M1, just as they were when read aloud in the drawing room a hundred years ago. Used and spoken intelligently, nothing can affect us more powerfully than words.

In Act IV of *The Tempest* Prospero conjures up a Masque, complete with Goddesses, dancing nymphs and reapers. A difficult production number to bring off magically, and not helped by the stage direction at the end: 'to a strange hollow and confused noise, they heavily vanish.' Difficult now, and with the technology of 1611, pretty impossible I should have thought. Immediately afterwards, Prospero speaks:

> You do look, my son, in a mov'd sort,
> As if you were dismay'd; be cheerful sir,
> Our revels now are ended, these our actors
> (As I foretold you) were all spirits, and
> Are melted into air, into thin air,
> And like the baseless fabric of this vision

The cloud-capped Towers, the gorgeous Palaces,
The solemn Temples, the great Globe itself,
Yea, all which it inherit, shall dissolve,
And like this insubstantial pageant faded
Leave not a rack behind: we are such stuff
As dreams are made on; and our little life
Is rounded with a sleep.

'I apologise for the Stage Management,' Shakespeare seems to be saying. 'It wasn't very magical, was it? Perhaps on the whole, the words do it better.'

Timothy West, CBE, FRSA
Chairman of LAMDA

INTRODUCTORY

EVERYBODY SAYS

Everybody says
I look just like my mother.
Everybody says
I'm the image of Aunt Bee.
Everybody says
My nose is like my father's
But *I* want to look like *ME!*

Dorothy Aldis

ONCE I SAW A LITTLE BIRD

Once I saw a little bird
Come hop, hop, hop!
So I cried: 'Little bird,
Will you stop, stop, stop?'

And was going to the window
To say, 'How do you do?'
But he shook his little tail
And away he flew.

Traditional

DORMOUSE

"Now winter is coming,"
The Dormouse said,
"I must be thinking
Of going to bed."
So he curled himself up
As small as he could,
And went fast asleep
As a dormouse should.

Lilian McCrea

SNOW PROBLEM

You can't make friends with a snowman,
So don't give one a cuddle,
Or you'll end up
With a wet shirt front
Standing in a puddle.

John Coldwell

GLOW-WORM

I know a worried glow-worm,
I wonder what the matter is?
He seems so glum and gloomy,
Perhaps he needs new batteries!

Colin West

DICKORY DOCK

Dickory Dock was a little grey mouse,
He ran here and there all over the house,
He ran on the mat, and he jumped on the chair -
In fact, he ran about everywhere,
He was up on the clock when it chimed out One
And didn't that Dickory Run-Run-Run.

Betty Pufford

GROUP INTRODUCTORY

FIVE LITTLE OWLS

Five little owls in an old elm tree,
Fluffy and puffy as owls could be,
Blinking and winking with big round eyes
As the big round moon that hung in the skies:
As I passed beneath, I could hear one say,
'There'll be mouse for supper, there will, today!'
Then all of them hooted, 'Tu-whit, Tu-whoo!
Yes, mouse for supper, Hoo hoo, Hoo hoo!'

Anon

JUMPING RHYME

Jump, jump, how high can you jump?
Up to the moon and down with a bump.

Skip, skip, how far can you skip?
All round the world with never a slip.

Hop, hop, how long can you hop?
From morning to night and never stop.

Run, run, how fast can you run?
On my two feet I chase the sun.

Sleep, sleep, how long will you sleep?
From morn to night in slumber deep.

Anne English

SONG OF THE WASHING MACHINE

Rolling them round,
Rolling them round,
Nothing else does it but
Rolling them round.

Swishing them clean,
Swishing them clean,
Some of those stockings
Weren't fit to be seen!

Spinning them dry,
Spinning them dry,
When you know how
It's as easy as pie!

When the job's over,
With nobody by it,
The Washing Machine
Is suddenly quiet.

Donald Mattam

JUNIOR PRELIMINARY

MUD

I like mud.
I like it on my clothes.
I like it on my fingers.
    I like it in my toes.

Dirt's pretty ordinary
    And dust's a dud.
For a really good mess-up
    I like mud.

John Smith

WHISPERS

Whispers
    tickle through your ear
    telling things you like to hear.

Whispers
    are as soft as skin
    letting little words curl in.

Whispers
    come so they can blow
    secrets others never know.

Myra Cohn Livingston

GROUP JUNIOR PRELIMINARY

WHO'S IN?

'The door is shut fast
    And everyone's out.'
But people don't know
    What they're talking about!
Say the fly on the wall,
And the flame on the coals,
And the dog on his rug,
And the mice in their holes,
And the kitten curled up,
And the spiders that spin -
    'What, everyone out?
    Why, everyone's in!'

Elizabeth Fleming

DUCK PARADE

See the little ducks come waddling down the lane -
    Waddle-waddle, quack! Waddle-waddle, quack!
Marching in the mud and paddling in the rain:
    Waddle-waddle, quack! Waddle-waddle, quack!
'We're going to the pond and we're never coming back again,
    Waddle-waddle, quack, quack, quack!'

But tea-time comes, and the little ducks complain:
    'Gobble, gobble, quack! Gobble-gobble, quack!'
Till out comes Jill with a bucket full of grain,
    Gobble, gobble, quack! Gobble-gobble, quack!
She rattles on her pail and they all waddle home again,
    Gobble, gobble, quack, quack, quack!

Clive Sansom

CARAVANS

I've seen caravans
Going to the fair!
    Come along,
    Come along;
Let's go there!

Hurrah! roundabouts
Lovely little swings,
    Coconuts,
    Coconuts,
Heaps of things!

See all the animals
Waiting for the show;
    Elephants,
    Elephants,
Let's all go!

Look! There's a tiger
Watching baby bears;
    Come away,
    Come away,
How he stares!

Hark! how the music plays
Ready for the fun!
    Come along,
    Come along,
Let's all run.

Irene Thompson

PRELIMINARY

GROUP PRELIMINARY

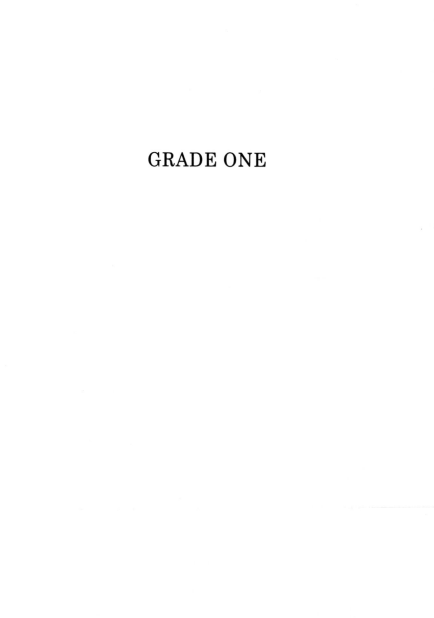

GRADE ONE

CHRISTMAS MORNING

Open the stocking,
what's in there?
Five hazelnuts, an apple,
a tangerine, a pear.

Untie the ribbons,
what do you spy?
A pencil and a hanky,
a freshly-baked mince pie.

Take off the wrappings,
what can it be?
A clockwork car, a storybook,
a game of chess for me.

Look by the fireside,
what is that?
A box of paints, a jigsaw,
a red wool stripy hat.

Peep through the curtains,
who goes there?
Mary and her Baby,
and the Christmas star.

Judith Nicholls

GRADE TWO

THE FLOWER-FED BUFFALOES

The flower-fed buffaloes of the spring
In the days of long ago,
Ranged where the locomotives sing
And the prairie flowers lie low:-
The tossing, blooming, perfumed grass
Is swept away by the wheat,
Wheels and wheels and wheels spin by
In the spring that still is sweet.
But the flower-fed buffaloes of the spring
Left us, long ago.
They gore no more, they bellow no more,
They trundle around the hills no more:-
With the Blackfeet, lying low,
With the Pawnees, lying low,
Lying low.

Vachel Lindsay

WHERE GO THE BOATS?

Dark brown is the river,
    Golden is the sand.
It flows along for ever,
    With trees on either hand.

Green leaves a-floating,
    Castles of the foam,
Boats of mine a-boating -
    Where will all come home?

On goes the river
    And out past the mill,
Away down the valley,
    Away down the hill.

Away down the river
A hundred miles or more,
Other little children
Shall bring my boats ashore.

Robert Louis Stevenson

COUNTING SHEEP

They said,
'If you can't get to sleep
try counting sheep.'
I tried.
It didn't work.

They said,
'Still awake? Count rabbits, dogs
or leaping frogs.'
I tried.
It didn't work.

They said,
'It's <u>VERY</u> late! Count rats,
or red-eyed bats!'
I tried.
It didn't work.

They said,
'Stop counting stupid sheep!
EYES CLOSED! DON'T PEEP!'
I tried.
And fell asleep.

Wes Magee

EVERY TIME I CLIMB A TREE

Every time I climb a tree
Every time I climb a tree
Every time I climb a tree
I scrape a leg
Or skin a knee
And every time I climb a tree
I find some ants
Or dodge a bee
And get the ants
All over me.

And every time I climb a tree
Where have you been?
They say to me
But don't they know that I am free
Every time I climb a tree?
I like it best
To spot a nest
That has an egg
Or maybe three.

And then I skin
The other leg
But every time I climb a tree
I see a lot of things to see
Swallows rooftops and TV
And all the fields and farms there be
Every time I climb a tree
Though climbing may be good for ants
It isn't awfully good for pants
But still it's pretty good for me
Every time I climb a tree.

David McCord

CHILD'S SONG IN SPRING

The silver birch is a dainty lady,
    She wears a satin gown;
The elm tree makes the old churchyard shady,
    She will not live in town.

The English oak is a sturdy fellow,
    He gets his green coat late;
The willow is smart in a suit of yellow,
    While brown the beech trees wait.

Such a gay green gown God gives the larches -
    As green as he is good!
The hazels hold up their arms for arches
    When Spring rides through the wood.

The chestnut's proud and the lilac's pretty,
    The poplar's gentle and tall,
But the plane tree's kind to the poor dull city -
    I love him best of all!

E. Nesbit

GRADE THREE

THE SLEEPY GIANT

My age is three hundred and seventy-two.
And I think, with the deepest regret,
How I used to pick up and voraciously chew
The dear little boys whom I met.
I've eaten them raw, in their holiday suits;
I've eaten them curried with rice;
I've eaten them baked, in their jackets and boots.
And found them exceedingly nice.

But now that my jaws are too weak for such fare,
I think it exceedingly rude
To do such a thing, when I'm quite well aware
Little boys do not like to be chewed.

And so I contentedly live upon eels,
And try to do nothing amiss.
And I pass all the time I can spare from my meals
In innocent slumber - like this.

Charles Edward Carryl

LOOK AT ALL THOSE MONKEYS

Look at all those monkeys
Jumping in their cage.
Why don't they all go out to work
And earn a decent wage?

How can you say such silly things,
And you a son of mine?
Imagine monkeys travelling on
The Morden-Edgware line!

But what about the Pekinese!
They have an allocation.
"Don't travel during Peke hour,"
It says on every station.

My Gosh, you're right, my clever boy,
I never thought of that!
And so they left the monkey house,
While an elephant raised his hat.

Spike Milligan

THE SHARK

The shark
Swims
In the dark
Of the deep
It's eye gleams
As it sees
Streams
Of gold fish -
Bold fish
Swimming too near
For the shark is well aware
That here
Is a tasty dish
Of fish
And the shark lies
In wait -
No fisherman,
No flies
No bait.
And the fish swim past
The shark follows,
Fast,
And swallows.

Lalla Ward

NOWHERE BEAR

I'm a nowhere bear, a threadbare bear,
A ruined bruin. Monsieur Misère
With a moth eaten coat, a buttony stare
And a bleat of a growl that's beyond repair...
Oh it isn't fair, it isn't fair,
I have my pride and I do still care
That I seem rather less than debonair,
So my only hope is I'll find somewhere
Before I surrender at last to despair
An old acquaintance, some kind confrère
From the days when we both had a lot more hair,
Who will take me up in his arms and declare -
You're a still very cuddly nowhere bear.

John Mole

WHO?

'Who,' asked my mother,
'helped themselves to the *new* loaf?'
    My two friends and I
    looked at her
    and shrugged.

'Who,'questioned my mother,
'broke off the crust?'
    Three pairs of eyes
    stared at the loaf
    lying on the kitchen table.

'Who,' demanded my mother,
'ate the bread?'
    No one replied.
    You could hear
    the kitchen clock. Tick. Tock.

And
even now I can taste it,
crisp, fresh, warm from the bakery,
    and I'd eat it again
    if I could find a loaf
    like that, like that...

Wes Magee

GRADE FOUR

THE SHADOW

When the last of gloaming's gone,
When the world is drowned in Night,
Then swims up the great round Moon,
Washing with her borrowed light
Twig, stone, grass-blade - pin-point bright -
Every tiniest thing in sight.

Then on tiptoe,
Off go I!
To a white-washed
Wall near by.

Where, for secret
Company,
My small shadow
Waits for me.

Still and stark,
Or stirring - *so*,
All I'm doing
He'll do too.

Quieter than
A cat he mocks
My walk, my gestures,
Clothes and locks.

I twist and turn,
I creep, I prowl,
Likewise does he,
The crafty soul,
The Moon for lamp,
And for music, owl.

"Sst" I whisper,
"Shadow, come!"
No answer:
He is blind and dumb -

Blind and dumb -
And when I go,
The wall will stand empty,
White as snow.

Walter de la Mare

THE BOGEYMAN

In the desolate depths of a perilous place
the bogeyman lurks, with a snarl on his face.
Never dare, never dare to approach his dark lair
for he's waiting ... just waiting ... to get you.

He skulks in the shadows, relentless and wild
in his search for a tender, delectable child.
With his steely sharp claws and his slavering jaws
oh he's waiting ... just waiting ... to get you.

Many have entered his dreary domain
but not even one has been heard from again.
They no doubt made a feast for the butchering beast
and he's waiting ... just waiting ... to get you.

In that sulphurous, sunless and sinister place
he'll crumple your bones in his bogey embrace.
Never never go near if you hold your life dear,
for oh! ... what he'll do ... when he gets you!

Jack Prelutsky

VEGETARIANS

Vegetarians are cruel unthinking people.
Everybody knows that a carrot screams when grated
That a peach bleeds when torn apart.
Do you believe an orange insensitive
to thumbs gouging out its flesh?
That tomatoes spill their brains
painlessly? Potatoes, skinned alive
and boiled, the soil's little lobsters.
Don't tell me it doesn't hurt
when peas are ripped from their overcoats,
the hide flayed off sprouts,
cabbage shredded, onions beheaded.

Throw in the trowel and lay down the hoe.
Mow no more. Let my people go!

Roger McGough

PATER'S BATHE

You can take a tub with a rub and a scrub in a two-foot tank of tin,
You can stand and look at the whirling brook and think about
    jumping in,
You can chatter and shake in the cold black lake, but the kind of
    bath for me,
Is to take a dip from the side of a ship, in the trough of the
    rolling sea.

You may lie and dream in the bed of a stream when an August day
    is dawning,
Or believe 'tis nice to break the ice on your tub of a winter
    morning,
You may sit and shiver beside the river, but the kind of bath for me
Is to take a dip from the side of a ship, in the trough of the
    rolling sea.

Edward Abbott Parry

THE PERFORMING BAG

The plastic bag that once was full
Of coloured sweets was empty and lost
And lay against the playground wall,
Flat and still among the dust.

But a wind came up the road,
Brushing back the hair of the grass,
Trying to unbutton people's coats
And teasing the leaves as it passed.

It felt its way inside the bag
Like a hand inside a glove
And like a puppet waking up
The plastic bag began to move.

As the air inside it puffed it out,
The bag that was lying sad and flat
Began to waggle its corners about
And nodded its head this way and that.

It dodged its way between the children
Who watched it carried high in the sky
And disappear on the hand of the wind
Waving them goodbye.

Stanley Cook

WHERE'S YOUR HOMEWORK?

As soon as I got home last night, Sir
I finished off my English homework first.
Put it on the kitchen table but my baby sister
found it. Chewed it and slavered all over it, Sir.
So I took it into the bath to check it through
like you asked us to do, Sir.
But reaching for the sponge

I dropped it in the bath.
It was so soggy that
I had to put the hair drier on it.
I burnt it to a crisp. Bone dry the paper was, Sir.
So I had a brainwave. I smeared Suntan lotion
on it to soften it up.
Left it for ten minutes
and the pages started to turn brown.

This morning I looked inside
and all the writing was smudged, Sir.
Could I have a new exercise book, please?

David Jackson

A WITCH'S SONG

Now I'm furnished for the flight,
Now I go, now I fly,
Malkin my sweet spirit and I.
O, what a dainty pleasure 'tis
To ride in the air
When the moon shines fair,
And sing and dance and toy and kiss.
Over woods, high rocks and mountains,
Over seas, our mistress' fountains,
Over steeples, towers, and turrets,
We fly by night, 'mongst troops of spirits.

No rings of bells to our ears sounds,
No howls of wolves, no yelp of hounds.
No, not the noise of water's breach,
Or cannon's throat can our height reach.

Thomas Middleton

ON THE TRAIN

When you go on the train
and the line goes past the backs of houses in a town
you can see there's thousands and thousands
of things going on;
someone's washing up,
a baby's crying,
someone's shaving,
someone said, 'Rubbish, I blame the government.'
someone tickled a dog
someone looked out the window
and saw this train
and saw me looking at her
and she thought,
'There's someone looking out the window
looking at me.'

But I'm only someone
looking out the window
looking at someone
looking out the window
looking at someone.

Then it's all gone.

Michael Rosen

THE FIR TREE

The candles were lighted. Oh, what a blaze of splendour! The Tree trembled in all his branches so that one of them caught fire. " Oh, dear!" cried the young lady, and it was extinguished in great haste.

So the Tree dared not tremble again; he was so fearful of losing something of his splendour, he felt almost bewildered in the midst of all this glory and brightness. And now, all of a sudden, both folding-doors were flung open, and a troop of children rushed in as if they had a mind to jump over him; the older people followed more quietly; the little ones stood quite silent, but only for a moment. Then their jubilee burst forth afresh, they shouted till the walls re-echoed; they danced round the Tree; one present after another was torn down.

"What are they doing?" thought the Tree; "what will happen now?" And the candles burned down to the branches; so they were extinguished, and the children were given leave to plunder the Tree. Oh! they rushed upon him in such riot that the boughs all crackled; had not his summit been festooned with the gold star to the ceiling, he would have been overturned.

Hans Andersen

JENNINGS GOES TO SCHOOL

Mr. Pemberton-Oakes decided that now would be the best time to test the boy's initiative. He would put him in charge of the fire drill and see what happened.

"Let us assume," he continued, "that instead of being half past two in the afternoon it is half past two in the morning, and a boy, in Dormitory Four - let us say Jennings, for example - awakens from sleep."

The mention of his name recalled Jennings from Lord's where in his imagination he had just put himself on to bowl at the pavilion end. He came to with a start.

"I beg your pardon, sir?" he said.

"I said, Jennings awakens from sleep," repeated the headmaster, "but judging from your appearance while I have been speaking, I was beginning to think you had gone into a state of hibernation for the winter. I trust that is not so?"

"I don't know, sir," replied Jennings. "I don't know what hiber - what you said - means, sir."

"It applies to such creatures as toads, moles, bats and, apparently, to some small boys," explained the headmaster. "Derived from the Latin word *hiberna* meaning winter quarters, it means - well, think, boy, think."

Jennings thought hard, but the atmosphere of Lord's still hung about him.

"Well, Jennings, what does a bat do in the winter?"

"It - er - splits if you don't oil it, sir," he said.

Anthony Buckeridge

MOONDIAL

Minty laughed despite herself. He was happier than she had ever seen him - carefree, as if he were on holiday. In a way, he was, she supposed. It seemed a shame to spoil it. But the menacing Miss Raven was on their track, and he must be warned. She tried again.

'No, Tom, listen! It's not Mrs Crump I mean, or Maggs - it's a woman from my time. She's -'

'Hey! Look! Look at that!' He let out a soft whistle. 'Ladies - with legs!'

A group of women was wandering up the path towards them, guide-books in hand.

'Where's their skirts? Oh my! Wait till I tell our Dorrie this!'

He started to caper towards them.

'Watch this!' he called. 'My turn to be invisible!'

Minty watched, horrorstruck. It was even more impossible that he should be invisible than it had seemed for herself to be. Surely they could see him?

But he was dancing about them now, making mock bows, pointing at their bare legs. Now he was thumbing his nose, waggling his fingers on his ears, pulling outrageous faces.

'It's so peaceful here!' sighed one of the party.

Minty giggled.

Helen Cresswell

THE MOUSE AND HIS CHILD

During the evening that followed the morning of the flag-raising, the elephant was observed to be deep in thought as she stood on the platform looking into the parlour, where the fluttering light of one dim candle alternately gained and lost its little territory in the shadows. 'Is anything troubling you, my dear?' the father asked.

'Not exactly troubling me,' said his wife. 'But the house seems to want something more, and I cannot for the life of me think what it is.'

'Another flagpole, Mama?' suggested the child.

'No,' said the elephant.

'Carpeting on the stairs?' said the seal.

'No,' said the elephant.

'Lights,' offered a quiet voice from the weeds below.

'Of course!' exclaimed the elephant. 'That's what it is! It's been so long since I lived indoors that I'd forgotten. This house used to have real lights, not just a few candle stubs.'

She paused. 'Who said that?' she asked.

Frog went to the edge of the platform and looked down. 'Manny Rat,' he said.

'Ugh!' said the elephant. 'I thought we had seen the last of that loathsome creature. Send him away.' The bittern launched himself from the platform, and the sometime boss of the dump cowered abjectly in the twilight among the weeds.

Russell Hoban

THE TALE OF JEREMY VOLE

The little dormouse started, lost his grip and fell into the leaves. He got up, ready to run. "Gosh! Jeremy, you scared me witless."

"So sorry," apologized the vole. "I wasn't sure it was you. Wet dormice are much of a much to me."

"Wet!" squeaked the dormouse. "I'm soaked to the skin! My nest washed away this morning and now I've nowhere to stay until I can patch together a new one."

"That is a problem," agreed Jeremy.

"AH-CHOOOT!" sneezed Morris. "And now I'm coming down with a cold." The big-eyed dormouse shivered and sniffed. With its long, fluffy fur all soaked down, the little creature looked like a soggy mop. "You'll have to excuse me - this is not turning out a very good day."

"I'm afraid you haven't seen the worst of it," Jeremy said.

"Do tell," sighed Morris. "What else?"

So Jeremy told the dripping dormouse all about the coming flood. Morris listened, sneezing now and then, and wringing his hands. "Well, I'm not surprised. Not at all. The way things have been going, I should have expected a flood would be next. Still, it's not as if I had a nice, warm nest to worry about."

"I'm sure you'll find another nest just as nice."

"Do you think so?" said Morris, brightening somewhat.

"Definitely," replied the vole.

Stephen Lawhead

THE REVENGE OF SAMUEL STOKES

Grandpa finished his sandwich and sat silent for a moment. "You'd have to go all out and cater for his tastes. Provide the sort of set-up he's used to - was used to."

"Such as?" enquired Jane.

"Let's see now. Eighteenth-century mansion grub? Well, I'm no expert but I reckon the sort of thing we'd have to lay on would be, um, peacock pie, a carp maybe, or roast pike, yes, roast pike would do if we could rustle one up. Syllabubs. Ales of one kind and another" - Grandpa's enthusiasm mounted - "I wonder if I could lay my hands on a guinea fowl? I suppose a swan might be overdoing it and you could get trouble with the Thames Conservancy people. Pigeon, possibly. A hare. That sort of thing."

The children were somewhat aghast. Jane said, "I'm not sure I like peacock pie. Not that I've ever had it."

"No beefburgers?"

"Definitely no beefburgers. D'you want the fellow to think we don't know what's what?"

Tim spotted a further difficulty. "How do we let him know it's happening? That it's specially for him?"

"I think," said Grandpa, "we may have to trust to luck there."

Penelope Lively

THE STORY OF KING ARTHUR

"Years ago," I began in a low voice, "my grandfather brought me here. It was here that he told me about you. He had already had the dream, you see, and he said that one day I would bring you here to find a magic sword. Tomorrow you shall have that sword and then I shall say goodbye and take my leave forever. My work in this world is done."

The young king clasped my hand. "Dear old friend, how can I say goodbye to you? I will never forget you. As long as I live, my people will honour the name of Merlin."

That night I slept a deep and dreamless sleep. I woke to see the lake glistening beneath the rising sun while a thin veil of early morning mist still clung to the reedy banks. Arthur was standing at the water's edge, transfixed. He was staring out at the lake. I followed his gaze and saw, through the mirror-smooth surface, a slender arm, holding a gleaming sword, which reached up towards the sky.

An old boat lay hidden in the reeds, where I remembered it. We waded to it and clambered in, soaked to the waist, then we paddled out towards the sword. As we approached we saw a woman smiling up at us through the gently rippled surface. Her black hair floated around her and her body shimmered in the water's dancing light. In her left hand was a silver scabbard, studded with precious stones.

I turned to my young companion. "Arthur, the sword is called Excalibur. It cuts through iron and steel and cannot break. Take it, it's yours."

Robin Lister

FIVE CHILDREN AND IT

Then Anthea cried out, '*I'm* not afraid. Let me dig,' and fell on her knees and began to scratch like a dog does when he has suddenly remembered where it was that he buried his bone.

'Oh, I felt fur,' she cried, half laughing and half crying. 'I did indeed! I did! when suddenly a dry husky voice in the sand made them all jump back, and their hearts jumped nearly as fast as they did.

'Let me alone,' it said. And now everyone heard the voice and looked at the others to see if they had too.

'But we want to see you,' said Robert bravely.

'I wish you'd come out,' said Anthea, also taking courage.

'Oh, well - if that's your wish,' the voice said, and the sand stirred and spun and scattered, and something brown and furry and fat came rolling out into the hole and the sand fell off it, and it sat there yawning and rubbing the ends of its eyes with its hands.

'I believe I must have dropped asleep,' it said, stretching itself.

The children stood around the hole in a ring, looking at the creature they had found. It was worth looking at. Its eyes were on long horns like a snail's eyes, and it could move them in and out like telescopes; it had ears like a bat's ears, and it's tubby body was shaped like a spider's and covered with thick soft fur; its legs and arms were furry too, and it had hands and feet like a monkey's.

'What on earth is it?' Jane said. 'Shall we take it home?'

E. Nesbit

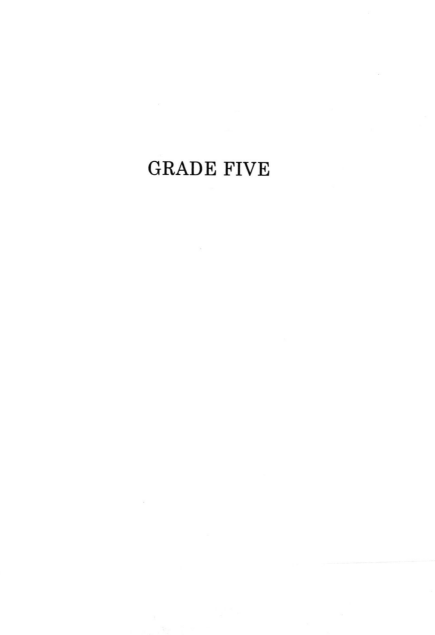

GRADE FIVE

SPRING BREEZES

The sudden shower has passed,
the spring breezes rustle

Blossoms of the cherry-apple
wake from sleep,
one petal dancing

By the rocks in the garden
the shimmering
heat waves rise

On the surface of the pond
a leaf boat
glides quietly along

I pray that
the spring breezes of good fortune
blow in the hearts of all

Daisaku Ikeda

THE WAY THROUGH THE WOODS

They shut the road through the woods
Seventy years ago.
Weather and rain have undone it again,
And now you would never know
There was once a road through the woods
Before they planted the trees.
It is underneath the coppice and heath,
And the thin anemones.
Only the keeper sees
That, where the ring-dove broods,
And the badgers roll at ease,
There was once a road through the woods.

Yet, if you enter the woods
Of a summer evening late,
When the night-air cools on the trout-ringed pools
Where the otter whistles his mate
(They fear not men in the woods
Because they see so few),
You will hear the beat of a horse's feet
And the swish of a skirt in the dew,
Steadily cantering through
The misty solitudes,
As though they perfectly knew
The old lost road through the woods ...
But there is no road through the woods!

Rudyard Kipling

THE TREES

The trees are coming into leaf
Like something almost being said;
The recent buds relax and spread,
Their greenness is a kind of grief.

Is it that they are born again
And we grow old? No, they die too.
Their yearly trick of looking new
Is written down in rings of grain.

Yet still the unresting castles thresh
In fullgrown thickness every May.
Last year is dead, they seem to say,
Begin afresh, afresh, afresh.

Philip Larkin

MOTHERS WHO DON'T UNDERSTAND

'Why can't you tidy your room?' they cry,
Millions of mothers who fret round the land,
'It's a horrible mess, I've never seen worse,'
- Mothers who don't understand.

They don't understand how cosy it is
To have piles of books on the floor,
And knickers and socks making friends with the vest
Under the bed, where *they* like it best,
And notices pinned to the door.

They don't understand why Kylie and Craig
Are smiling all over the walls,
And toffees and Chewys and dozens of Smarties
Are scattered about reminding of parties,
And jeans are rolled into balls.

They don't understand why a good bed should be
All scrumpled and friendly and gritty,
Why the bears and the paints and the toys are much less
Easy to find if there *isn't* a mess -
To tidy would be a great pity.

They don't understand the point of a desk
Is to balance the muddle quite high:
To leave the drawers open, grow mould on the drink,
Is very much easier, some people think,
Than explaining to mothers just why.

'PLEASE can you tidy your room?' they wail,
Millions of mothers who fret round the land:
'What will you do when there's no one to nag you?'
- Mothers who don't understand.

Augusta Skye

GREEN MAN, BLUE MAN

As I was walking through Guildhall Square
I smiled to see a green man there,
But when I saw him coming near
My heart was filled with nameless fear.

As I was walking through Madford Lane
A blue man stood there in the rain.
I asked him in by my front-door,
For I'd seen a blue man before.

As I was walking through Landlake Wood
A grey man in the forest stood,
But when he turned and said, 'Good day'
I shook my head and ran away.

As I was walking by Church Stile
A purple man spoke there a while.
I spoke to him because, you see,
A purple man once lived by me.

But when the night falls dark and fell
How, O how, am I to tell,
Grey man, green man, purple, blue,
Which is which is which of you?

Charles Causley

CARGOES

Quinquireme of Nineveh from distant Ophir
Rowing home to haven in sunny Palestine,
With a cargo of ivory,
And apes and peacocks,
Sandalwood, cedarwood, and sweet white wine.

Stately Spanish galleon coming from the Isthmus,
Dipping through the Tropics by the palm-green shores,
With a cargo of diamonds,

THE LION AND THE MOUSE

A lion was awakened from a very satisfying sleep by a cheeky mouse running over his face. Rising up in anger, he caught him and was about to kill him when the mouse cried out: 'If you only spare my life, I will surely be able to repay your kindness one day.'

The lion laughed at the idea of a mere mouse ever being able to help him, but because it was a nice day he decided to let him go free. It so happened that shortly after this the lion was caught by some hunters, who bound him with strong ropes and tied him to the ground. The lion roared and roared with anger, and the mouse, recognizing his voice, came up and gnawed through the ropes with his sharp teeth. When the lion was free, the mouse said to him: 'You laughed when I said that one day I would be able to help you. But now you know that sometimes it is possible for even a mouse to help a lion.'

Aesop

THE INCREDIBLE JOURNEY

Down the trail, out of the darkness of the bush and into the light of the slanting bars of sunlight, joggling along with his peculiar nautical roll, came - Ch. Boroughcastle Brigadier of Doune.

Boroughcastle Brigadier's ragged banner of a tail streamed out behind him, his battle-scarred ears were upright and for-ward, and his noble pink and black nose twitched, straining to encompass all that his short gaze was denied. Thin and tired, hopeful, happy - and hungry, his remarkable face alight with expectation - the old warrior was returning from the wilderness. Bodger, beautiful for once, was coming as fast as he could.

He broke into a run, faster and faster, until the years fell away, and he hurled himself towards Peter.

And as he had never run before, as though he would out-distance time, Peter was running towards his dog.

John Longridge turned away, then, and left them, an indistinguishable tangle of boy and dog, in a world of their own making. He started down the trail as in a dream, his eyes unseeing.

Halfway down he became aware of a small animal running at lightning speed towards him. It swerved past his legs with an agile twist and he caught a brief glimpse of a black-masked face and a long black tail before it disappeared up the trail in the swiftness of a second.

It was Tao, returning for his old friend, that they might end their journey together.

Sheila Burnford

CARRIE'S WAR

Hepzibah's power? Did he mean Hepzibah was a witch, then? Albert had said that she was! Carrie stood shivering in the cold hall behind the half open door, wondering about Hepzibah and remembering her spell-binding voice telling that story about the old skull. And then felt, suddenly, that she was all the things Nick had said. A traitor, a mean, dirty traitor, standing here and listening and letting Mr Evans go on thinking that she hadn't liked Hepzibah. That she hadn't been taken in, was what he had said! Well she would put that right now, this minute! March in and tell him, straight to his face! She drew a deep breath and ran into the kitchen and they turned in their chairs to look at her. Auntie Lou guiltily; Mr Evans with the angry red coming up in his face.

'What are you doing, girl? You went to bed, didn't you? Up and down, up and down, tramp, tramp, tramp on the carpet!'

'I walked on the paint,' Carrie said, but his face was almost purple by now and the veins stood out on his forehead as he half rose from his chair.

'Up and down, up and down, I won't have it, see? Back up with you now, double quick!' And as Carrie fled, his ranting voice followed her. 'Up and down, back and for, in and out, messing and humbugging about...'

Nina Bawden

CATWEAZLE

Carrot walked miserably across the room and turning at the door, made one last attempt to speak.

'Go to bed!' ordered his father, convinced that Carrot was just trying to be funny, and the boy slunk out of the room.

'Ain't never seen 'im like that before,' said Sam. Mr Bennet sighed heavily. 'When I was in the army,' he said, 'we called that dumb insolence.'

There was a sudden gobbling from one of the turkey pens. The two men listened.

'Could be a fox,' said Sam.

It wasn't a fox. It was Catweazle looking for somewhere to hide for the night. He shied away from the strange birds and their unearthly cries and eventually found refuge in a disused chicken coop, on the edge of the farm. Creeping in and carefully shutting the door behind him, he examined his new shelter.

Hanging from the roof was an old hurricane lantern, so Catweazle looked on the door post for a switch. As chance would have it there was a large nail sticking out at an angle, and he crooked his finger round it and looking towards the lantern, gave a tug.

'Shine tiny sun,' he chanted, pulling on the nail. 'Shine tiny sun!' Nothing happened. There was no blinding light to dazzle him and after trying again for a few times he gave up.

Richard Carpenter

THE ANIMALS OF FARTHING WOOD

As he sped back towards the camp in the gorse thicket, and in the direction of the flames, Fox resolutely put every fearsome thought from his mind. He told himself to think only of Toad, and how he must save him to save the others. Without Toad they were indeed lost.

The fire grew brighter and noisier ahead of him, and soon the air smelt, and felt, hot and scorched. The heat increased continually. There was no sign of Toad.

Fox began to call him. 'Toad! Toad! Where are you?' Then, raising his voice above the noise of the burning, he shouted as loudly as he could: 'TOAD!'

Fox dared not look directly at the terrifying sight that he was swiftly approaching. He knew that to do so would mean an instantaneous loss of nerve. But he could hear the crashing of blazing boughs - sometimes whole saplings. The roar of the greedy flames was hideous, and at last he could go no further. His courage failed him, and he felt all he could do was turn and run back to safety and companionship.

Then he heard a desperate croak. 'Fox! Have you come back? Here I am!'

Colin Dann

WHITE FANG

White Fang turned to the love-master's wife. She screamed with fright as he seized her dress in his teeth and dragged on it till the frail fabric tore away. By this time he had become the centre of interest. He had ceased from his growling, and stood, head up, looking into their faces. His throat worked spasmodically, but made no sound, while he struggled with all his body, convulsed with the effort to rid himself of the incommunicable something that strained for utterance.

'I hope he is not going mad,' said Weedon's mother. 'I told Weedon that I was afraid the warm climate would not agree with an Arctic animal.'

'He's trying to speak, I do believe,' Beth announced.

At this moment speech came to White Fang, rushing up in a great burst of barking.

'Something has happened to Weedon,' his wife said decisively.

They were all on their feet now, and White Fang ran down the steps, looking back for them to follow. For the second and last time in his life he had barked and made himself understood.

Jack London

THE HOBBIT

'It's got to ask uss a quesstion, my preciouss, yes, yess, yesss. Just one more question to guess, yes, yess,' said Gollum.

But Bilbo simply could not think of any question with that nasty wet cold thing sitting next to him, and pawing and poking him. He scratched himself, he pinched himself: still he could not think of anything.

'Ask us! Ask us!' said Gollum.

Bilbo pinched himself and slapped himself; he gripped on his little sword; he even felt in his pocket with his other hand. There he found the ring he had picked up in the passage and forgotten about.

'What have I got in my pocket?' he said aloud. He was talking to himself, but Gollum thought it was a riddle, and he was frightfully upset.

'Not fair! Not fair!' he hissed. 'It isn't fair, my precious, is it, to ask us what it's got in its nassty little pocketses?'

Bilbo seeing what had happened and having nothing better to ask stuck to his question, 'What have I got in my pocket?' he said louder.

'S-s-s-s-s,' hissed Gollum. 'It must give us three guesseses, my preciouss, three guesseses.'

'Very well! Guess away!' said Bilbo.

'Handses!' said Gollum.

'Wrong,' said Bilbo, who had luckily just taken his hand out again. 'Guess again!'

J.R.R. Tolkien

THE BIRTHDAY OF THE INFANTA

Now when the little Dwarf heard that he was to dance a second time before the Infanta, and by her own express command, he was so proud that he ran out into the garden, kissing the white rose in an absurd ecstasy of pleasure, and making the most uncouth and clumsy gestures of delight.

The Flowers were quite indignant at his daring to intrude into their beautiful home, and when they saw him capering up and down the walks, and waving his arms above his head in such a ridiculous manner, they could not restrain their feelings any longer.

'He is really far too ugly to be allowed to play in any place where we are,' cried the Tulips.

'He should drink poppy-juice, and go to sleep for a thousand years,' said the great scarlet Lilies, and they grew quite hot and angry.

'He is a perfect horror!' screamed the Cactus. 'Why, he is twisted and stumpy, and his head is completely out of proportion with his legs. Really he makes me feel prickly all over, and if he comes near me I will sting him with my thorns.'

'And he has actually got one of my best blooms,' exclaimed the white Rose-tree. 'I gave it to the Infanta this morning myself, as a birthday present, and he has stolen it from her.' And she called out: 'Thief, thief, thief!' at the top of her voice.

Oscar Wilde

GRADE SIX

THE INSULT

I have been insulted.
My feelings have been hurt
And I am not coming back into the house.
You laughed at me.
Don't think that I was fooled.
You weren't laughing *with* me
But AT me
When I lost my balance
Washing,
And fell over.
You laughed,
And it wasn't funny.
All my grace, control, and dignity were gone;
You robbed me of my image of myself
And with your braying
All but destroyed my pride.
Don't think I cannot take a joke.
There's nothing lacking with my sense of humour,
I just don't like being made to look ridiculous.
It's no use your standing there calling,
'Kitty, kitty, kitty!'
Or offering me bribes.
Your coarse laughter
Has offended me deeply
And it may take me some time to get over it,
Or never.
If and when I come back at all
It will be
In my own sweet time.

Paul Gallico

VOLCANO

Under the cold ash-peak,
under a crown of fitful flowers,
he sleeps,

under the silent crust,
welded and twisted from ancient meanders
and bitter lakes of fluid rock,
he sleeps.

Coiled, black, hissing,
curled, dark, hissing,
waiting while time whirls slowly past.

(A thousand years
in the blink of a slow stone eye.)

Rain washes his back,
smoothing mud into the crevices,
helping grass to dress him in summer clothing.

Trees clutch him with fingered roots,
But never deep enough to spoil his sleep,
Never deep enough to ruffle his hot dreams.

But once upon a time, just as a soft summer
is folding itself into autumn,
his hiss becomes a roar,
His skin cracks and stretches,
His black jaws open in a vast and fiery yawn.

The surprised grass crackles and blackens,
and floats away;
Trees wave like torches and dissolve;
His skin heaves and splits,
folds and breaks
as the snake swiftly rises,
and tumbles and rumbles
into the broken and burning valley.

THE SERPENT

There was a Serpent who had to sing.
There was. There was.
He simply gave up Serpenting.
Because. Because.

He didn't like his Kind of Life;
He couldn't find a proper Wife;
He was a Serpent with a soul;
He got no Pleasure down his Hole.
And so, of course, he had to Sing,
And Sing he did, like Anything!
The Birds, they were, they were Astounded;
And various Measures Propounded
To stop the Serpent's Awful Racket:
They bought a Drum. He wouldn't Whack it.
They sent, - you always send, - to Cuba
And got a Most Commodious Tuba;
They got a Horn, they got a Flute,
But Nothing would suit.
He said, 'Look, Birds, all this is futile:
I do not like to Bang or Tootle.'
And then he cut loose with a Horrible Note
That practically split the Top of his Throat.
'You see,' he said, with a Serpent's Leer,
'I'm Serious about my Singing Career!'
And the Woods Resounded with many a Shriek
As the Birds flew off to the End of Next Week.

Theodore Roethke

WINTER

When icicles hang by the wall,
And Dick the shepherd blows his nail,
And Tom bears logs into the hall,
And milk comes frozen home in pail,
When blood is nipp'd, and ways be foul,
Then nightly sings the staring owl:
'Tu-who;
Tu-whit, Tu-who'- A merry note,
While greasy Joan doth keel the pot.

When all aloud the wind doth blow,
And coughing drowns the parson's saw,
And birds sit brooding in the snow,
And Marian's nose looks red and raw,
When roasted crabs hiss in the bowl,
Then nightly sings the staring owl:
'Tu-who;
Tu-whit, Tu-who'- A merry note,
While greasy Joan doth keel the pot.

William Shakespeare

THE DARK IS RISING

'You are the Sign-seeker, Will Stanton. That is your destiny, your first quest. If you can accomplish that, you will have brought to life one of the three great forces that the Old Ones must turn soon towards vanquishing the powers of the Dark, which are reaching out now steadily and stealthily over all this world.'

The rhythms of his voice, which had been rising and falling in an increasingly formal pattern, changed subtly into a kind of chanted battle cry; a call, Will thought suddenly, with a chill tightening his skin, to things beyond the great hall and beyond the time of the calling. 'For the Dark, the Dark is rising. The Walker is abroad, the Rider is riding; they have woken, the Dark is rising. And the last of the Circle is come to claim his own, and the circles must now all be joined. The white horse must go to the Hunter, and the river take the valley; there must be fire on the mountain, fire under the stone, fire over the sea. Fire to burn away the Dark, for the Dark, the Dark is rising!'

He stood there tall as a tree in the shadowed room, his deep voice ringing out in an echo, and Will could not take his eyes from him. *The Dark is rising.* That was exactly what he had felt last night. That was what he was beginning to feel again now, a shadowy awareness of evil pricking at his fingertips and the top of his spine, but for the life of him he could not utter a word.

Susan Cooper

THE NEVER-ENDING STORY

The sound of his voice had hardly died away when a pearly-white luckdragon rose from the hollow where the gnomes had their cave and flew through the air with lazy, sinuous movements. He must have been feeling playful, for now and then he turned over on his back and looped-the-loop so fast that he looked like a burst of white flame. And then he landed not far from the pyramid where Atreyu was standing. When he propped himself on his forepaws, he was so high above Atreyu that to bring his head close to him, he had to bend his long, supple neck sharply downward. Rolling his ruby-red eyeballs for joy, stretching his tongue far out of his wide-open gullet, he boomed in his bronze-bell voice: 'Atreyu, my friend and master! So you've finally come back! I'm so glad! We had almost given up hope - the gnomes, that is, not I.'

'I'm glad too!' said Atreyu. 'But what has happened in this one night?'

'One night?' cried Falkor. 'Do you think it's been only one night? You're in for a surprise. Climb on, I'll carry you.'

Atreyu swung himself up on the enormous animal's back. It was his first time aboard a luckdragon. And though he had ridden wild horses and was anything but timid, this first short ride through the air took his breath away.

Michael Ende

GOGGLE-EYES

Mum laughed.

'Oh, dear, Kitty. Looks like, if Gerald gets his way, you've had your chips!'

I suppose, looking back, she only intended it as some harmless little potato joke. But I must say I didn't find it funny. I felt humiliated, standing there with muddy hands, while those two stood arm in arm beside the sink, grinning.

On any other day, I would have lost my temper. I would have forgotten my promise, and yelled at him to push off with his Goggle-eyes, stop sticking his nose into other people's business, clear out, go *home*!

But, that day, I'd been feeling so *happy*. All the way to the library, and all the way home, the world had suddenly seemed so huge and colourful, the wind so puffy and fresh, the skies so high.

To come home in such tremendous spirits and pull Dad's heavy spade out of the shed to dig up spuds for Mum because I love her and she was happy today, too - and then to come through the door and, within seconds, find that the carping had begun again ...

Well, it was all too much. I burst out crying. To be quite honest, I didn't even *burst*. I just began to cry, like a baby. Tears pricked behind my eyes, and before I could stop them - before I could even spin round and rush out of the room - they'd welled up and over, spilled down my cheeks, and splashed like ink blots on my muddy shoes.

Anne Fine

BAMBI'S CHILDREN

For the first time Geno noticed that the morning did not get brighter as it should. There was a darkness in the sky, a new and livid colour of dark that seemed to bring the treetops closer to the ground, and that seemed to be filled with the scent of sulphur and a great humming force.

Now the other trees began to tremble in the order of their size: the tall elms first, the maples and the oaks that shivered on their sturdy trunks, and then all of them were trembling, their dry leaves shaking and sometimes falling, spiralling, to earth.

Geno was afraid. Like the trees, he shivered also. He woke Faline in fear.

"Mother!" he cried urgently. "Wake up, Mother! Something terrible is going to happen!"

Then came the rain.

It came like lances hurled by an evil host. It beat with a loud drumming in the trees. It hurled itself on the lesser plants pressing them down. It was dark as night until the thunder came.

A bolt of lightning tore the sky. It lighted the tortured trees, it lighted the hidden avenues where nothing moved. It flashed also on Bambi, standing before them like the spirit of the storm, his great antlers proud against it, his coat aflame with fire reflected in the rain. He trumpeted, piercing the mêlée of the storm:

'Don't be afraid, nothing will hurt you! Faline, avoid the higher trees, above all the poplar. Keep among the outer bushes of the wood!'

Lightning and thunder died. Darkness returned. They could not see him, but they knew that he had gone.

Felix Salten

THE CRICKET IN TIMES SQUARE

The next morning, which was the last Sunday in August, all three Bellinis came to open the newsstand. They could hardly believe what had happened yesterday and were anxious to see if Chester would continue to sing familiar songs. Mario gave the cricket his usual breakfast of mulberry leaves and water, which Chester took his time eating. He could see that everyone was very nervous and he sort of enjoyed making them wait. When breakfast was over, he had a good stretch and limbered his wings.

Since it was a Sunday, Chester thought it would be nice to start with a hymn, so he chose to open his concert with 'Rock of Ages.' At the sound of the first notes, the faces of Mama and Papa and Mario broke into smiles. They looked at each other and their eyes told how happy they were, but they didn't dare to speak a word.

During the pause after Chester had finished 'Rock of Ages,' Mr Smedley came up to the newsstand to buy his monthly copy of *Musical America*. His umbrella, neatly folded, was hanging over his arm as usual.

"Hey, Mr Smedley - my cricket plays hymns!" Mario blurted out even before the music teacher had a chance to say good morning.

"And opera!" said Papa.

"And Italian songs!" said Mama.

"Well, well, well," said Mr. Smedley, who didn't believe a word, of course. "I see we've all become very fond of our cricket. But aren't we letting our imaginations run away with us a bit?"

"Oh no," said Mario. "Just listen. He'll do it again."

George Selden

THE SWISS FAMILY ROBINSON

I now woke the children. Fritz sprang nimbly out of the tent, while his little brothers began to gape and rub their eyes, to get rid of their sleepiness. Fritz ran to visit his jackal, which during the night had become cold and perfectly stiff. He fixed him upon his legs, and placed him to look like a sentinel at the entrance of the tent, joyously expecting the wonder and acclamations of his little brothers at so singular and unexpected an appearance. But no sooner had the dogs caught a sight of him than they began a horrible barking, and set themselves in motion to fall upon him instantly, thinking he was alive. Fritz had enough to do to restrain them, and succeeded only by dint of coaxing and perseverance. In the meantime their barking had effectually awakened the younger boys, and they all ran out of the tent, curious to know what could be the occasion. Jack was the first who appeared, with the young monkey on his shoulders; but when the little creature perceived the jackal, he sprang away in terror, and hid himself at the farthest extremity of the grass which composed our bed.

The children were much surprised at the sight of a yellow-coloured animal standing without motion at the entrance of the tent.

'Oh, dear!' exclaimed Francis: 'it is a wolf!'

'No, no,' said Jack, going near the jackal and taking one of his paws; 'it is a yellow dog, and he is dead.'

'It is neither a dog nor a wolf,' put in Ernest. 'Do you not see that it is a golden fox?'

Johann Wyss

CHILDREN ON THE OREGON TRAIL

He had reached the top. He made his last steps slowly, very slowly. He looked down over the other side. He saw ...

That ... that was impossible! How could it be, so - so suddenly? It was such a wonderful sight, what he saw there. So splendid, so unbelievable, so ... it must be an optical illusion, he thought. He shook his head and shut his eyes. Then he opened them again. He looked at Indepentia, he looked down ... it was *not* an optical illusion, it was what he had been hungering for all those weeks, and now that it was there he could not believe it.

Far below him, far below this last chain of the Blue Mountains, lay a wide, long, green valley, with trees and shrubs still clad in their autumn yellow. There were the small square shapes of a few log cabins, a thin plume of smoke rose from a chimney - it was the mission station of Dr Marcus Whitman. It was Oregon; it must be the Columbia valley. Down there he saw a winding, silver ribbon with edges of luxuriant green.

Great Father in Heaven, they were there!

He did not look round at the others. He did not beckon and he did not wave; he did not shout. He stood motionless, gazing down, and let them come.

A. Rutgers van der Loeff

HAPHAZARD HOUSE

Stillness. We gathered close together in the road. I had never experienced stillness. The quiet was awesome. My tired ears, full of the sound of traffic and the Mini's engine, took a while to adjust.

Then I heard the cooling engines click, and Victoria sigh. There was a full moon. The shadow of a church tower fell across our group. The church clock ticked, the minute hand jerked, the clock whirred, then struck twice.

The square was small; four roads led from it. On tiptoe Josh and I explored. There was a post office and general store, and that was all in the way of shops. The village was very small, the church of cathedral proportions. We went back to the others.

'Which way now?' Even Grandpa didn't speak above a whisper.

'I don't know.' Pa tipped the hat to the back of his head.

'We cannot wake anybody at this hour,' whispered Ma.

'Why not?' Grandpa looked worn out.

'Darling, just look at us.' Ma grinned. I could see her teeth in the moonlight. 'We'd make an awful impression. We look like a pop festival in this van. Or refugees.'

'Maybe, but we must ask where Haphazard is. We can't spend the rest of the night here.'

Mary Wesley

GRADE SEVEN

YOUNG LAMBS

The spring is coming by a many signs;
The trays are up, the hedges broken down
That fenced the haystack, and the remnant shines
Like some old antique fragment weathered brown.
And where suns peep, in every sheltered place,
The little early buttercups unfold
A glittering star or two - till many trace
The edges of the blackthorn clumps in gold.
And then a little lamb bolts up behind
The hill, and wags his tail to meet the yoe;[*]
And then another, sheltered from the wind,
Lies all his length as dead - and lets me go
Close by, and never stirs, but basking lies,
With legs stretched out as though he could not rise.

John Clare

THE CHURCH MOUSE

Here in a crumbled corner of the wall,
Well stockt with food from harvest festival,
My twitching ears and delicate small snout
And velvet feet that know their way about
From age to age in snug contentment dwell,
Unseen, and serve my hungry nestlings well.

The slanting light makes patterns on the floor
Of nave and chancel. At my kitchen door
God's acre stretches greenly, should I wish
To take the air and seek a daintier dish.
And week by week the shuddering organ mews,
And all my world is filled with boots and shoes.

* Yoe: ewe

Sometimes, on Sundays, from my living tomb
I venture out into the vast room,
Smelling my way, as pious as you please,
Among the hassocks and the bended knees,
To join with giants, being filled with food,
In worship of the Beautiful, the Good:
The all-creative Incorporeal Mouse,
Whose radiant odours warm this holy house.

Gerald Bullett

WHEN I HAVE FEARS THAT I MAY CEASE TO BE

When I have fears that I may cease to be
    Before my pen has gleaned my teeming brain,
Before high-piled books, in charactery,
    Hold like rich garners the full-ripen'd grain;
When I behold, upon the night's starred face,
    Huge cloudy symbols of a high romance,
And think that I may never live to trace
    Their shadows, with the magic hand of chance;
And when I feel, fair creature of an hour,
    That I shall never look upon thee more,
Never have relish in the faery power
    Of unreflecting love; - then on the shore
Of the wide world I stand alone, and think
Till love and fame to nothingness do sink.

John Keats

BACK FROM AUSTRALIA

Cocooned in Time at this inhuman height
    The packaged food tastes neutrally of clay.
    We never seem to catch the running day
But travel on in everlasting night

With all the chic accoutrements of flight:
    Lotions and essences in neat array
    And yet another plastic cup and tray.
'Thank you *so* much. Oh no, I'm quite all right.'

At home in Cornwall hurrying autumn skies
    Leave Bray Hill barren, Stepper jutting bare,
      And hold the moon above the sea-wet sand.
The very last of late September dies
    In frosty silence and the hills declare
      How vast the sky is, looked at from the land.

John Betjeman

THE RHODORA

In May, when sea-winds pierced our solitudes,
I found the fresh Rhodora in the woods,
Spreading its leafless blooms in a damp nook,
To please the desert and the sluggish brook.
The purple petals, fallen in the pool,
Made the black water with their beauty gay;
Here might the red-bird come his plumes to cool,
And court the flowers that cheapen his array.

Rhodora! if the sages ask thee why
This charm is wasted on the earth and sky,
Tell them, dear, that if eyes were made for seeing,
Then Beauty is its own excuse for being:
Why thou wert there, O rival of the rose!
I never thought to ask, I never knew:
But in my simple ignorance, suppose
The self-same Power that brought me there brought you.

Ralph Waldo Emerson

MEMORIAL TABLET

(War of 1914-18)

Squire nagged and bullied till I went to fight
(Under Lord Derby's scheme). I died in hell -
(They called it Passchendaele); my wound was slight,
And I was hobbling back, and then a shell
Burst slick upon the duck-boards; so I fell
Into the bottomless mud, and lost the light.

In sermon-time, while Squire is in his pew,
He gives my gilded name a thoughtful stare;
For though low down upon the list, I'm there:
'In proud and glorious memory' - that's my due.
Two bleeding years I fought in France for Squire;
I suffered anguish that he's never guessed;
Once I came home on leave; and then went west.
What greater glory could a man desire?

Siegfried Sassoon

BOY AT THE WINDOW

Seeing the snowman standing all alone
In dusk and cold is more than he can bear.
The small boy weeps to hear the wind prepare
A night of gnashings and enormous moan.
His tearful sight can hardly reach to where
The pale-faced figure with bitumen eyes
Returns him such a god-forsaken stare
As outcast Adam gave to Paradise.

The man of snow is, nonetheless, content,
Having no wish to go inside and die.
Still, he is moved to see the youngster cry.
Though frozen water is his element,
He melts enough to drop from one soft eye

A trickle of the purest rain, a tear
For the child at the bright pane surrounded by
Such warmth, such light, such love, and so much fear.

Richard Wilbur

THE SPRING

Now that the Winter's gone, the earth hath lost
Her snow-white robes, and now no more the frost
Candies the grass, or casts an icy cream
Upon the silver lake or crystal stream:
But the warm sun thaws the benumbed earth,
And makes it tender, gives a sacred birth
To the dead swallow: wakes in hollow tree
The drowsy cuckoo and the humble-bee.
Now do a choir of chirping minstrels bring
In triumph to the world, the youthful Spring.
The valleys, hills, and woods in rich array
Welcome the coming of the long'd for May.
Now all things smile: only my Love doth lour;
Nor hath the scalding noonday sun the power
To melt that marble ice, which still doth hold
Her heart congealed, and makes her pity cold.
The ox, which lately did for shelter fly
Into the stall, doth now securely lie
In open fields; and love no more is made
By the fireside, but in the cooler shade
Amyntas now doth with his Chloris sleep
Under a sycamore, and all things keep
Time with the season: only she doth carry
June in her eyes, in her heart January.

Thomas Carew

MY UNCLE SILAS

My Uncle Silas was a man who could eat anything. He could eat stewed nails. He had lived on them, once, for nearly a week. He told me so.

I was a boy then. At that time we used to drive over to see him, in summer, about one Sunday a month, arriving in time for dinner, tethering the white horse about noon in the shade of the big Pearmain overhanging the lane outside. It was always what were we going to eat and what were we going to wet with? At dinner, once, we had pheasant, which was something very special, and I asked him if he had shot it. 'No,' he said, 'it just fell down the chimney.' Another time we had a goose and I asked him if that fell down the chimney. 'No,' he said, 'it was sittin' on eighteen eggs in the winter oats and I cut its two legs off wi' the scythe. Cut 'em off and never broke egg. Ain't that right, George?'

'Yes, that's right,' my grandfather said.

'Well it ain't, then,' Silas said, cocking his bloodshot eye at him. 'Don't you go tellin' the kid such blamed lies. Cut the goose's legs off wi' the scythe! -tck! tck! tck! tck! Don't you believe it, boy. It's just his tale. He's just stuffin' you. The goose went to sleep in the well-bucket and I went to draw some water one night and let it down unbeknownst and it got drowned.'

'Couldn't it swim?' I said.

'Oh! it was asleep. Never woke. It just went a belly-flopper and was done for.'

H.E. Bates

GEORGE SILVERMAN'S EXPLANATION

A worldly little devil was my mother's usual name for me. Whether I cried for that I was in the dark, or for that it was cold, or for that I was hungry, or whether I squeezed myself into a warm corner when there was a fire, or ate voraciously when there was food, she would still say, " Oh you worldly little devil!" And the sting of it was, that I quite well knew myself to be a worldly little devil. Worldly as to wanting to be housed and warmed, worldly as to wanting to be fed, worldly as to the greed with which I inwardly compared how much I got of those good things with how much my father and mother got, when, rarely, those good things were going.

Sometimes they both went away seeking work; and then I would be locked up in the cellar for a day or two at a time. I was at my worldliest then. Left alone, I yielded myself up to a worldly yearning for enough of anything (except misery), and for the death of my mother's father, who was a machine-maker at Birmingham, and on whose decease, I had heard mother say, she would come into a whole courtful of houses "if she had her rights." Worldly little devil, I would stand about, musingly fitting my cold bare feet into cracked bricks and crevices of the damp cellar-floor, walking over my grandfather's body, so to speak, into the courtful of houses, and selling them for meat and drink, and clothes to wear.

Charles Dickens

THE MOON OF GOMRATH

Susan stared so hard all around her that the blackness seemed to be spotted with light - pale flecks of green; and then she noticed that, instead of swimming in rainbow patterns, as such lights do when the eyes strain against darkness, these lights did not change colour, but were grouped close to the ground, motionless, in pairs. They were eyes. She was surrounded by a field of green, unwinking, hard eyes - every one fixed on her.

The cats closed in. Now Susan could see them as individuals: there were two or three dozen of them, and they walked stifflegged and bristling. Susan was too frightened to move, even as they approached, until one of the cats hissed, and lunged at her with its claws. Before she had time to realise that the blow would not have touched her, Susan jumped in the opposite direction, and here the cats gave way and made a green passage for her, and their intention was plain. She found that she could move freely where they wished her to go, but if she veered from that line or tried to stop, claws were unsheathed.

She knew that whatever the danger was that Cadellin had feared, these cats were part of it: there was too much intelligence in their movements for them to be ordinary cats, and that was the least strange aspect of them.

So for a while, just as had happened earlier with Colin, Susan was herded through the wood. The cats did not touch her, but they walked close, and urged her to run: and this eagerness showed Susan her weapon against them.

Alan Garner

RICE WITHOUT RAIN

'I had thought that I would start by introducing each of us to you,' the stranger said, and his gaze seemed to seek Jinda out and focus on her even though she was at the very edge of the crowd. 'But now I think that perhaps the best way to start, unusual as it may be, is to sing to you a song which would tell you about us better than any words can.'

He smiled, and to Jinda it seemed as if he was smiling directly at her. Then, taking a deep breath, he began to sing.

His voice was slow and deliberate, almost a chant, and in the stillness it spiralled up to the trees canopying the fire. One by one, hesitantly at first and then with more vigour, the three other strangers joined him in song, until it seemed as if the song was surging forth from the night itself.

Jinda hugged her knees to her and listened, entranced. She had never heard anything like this in her life, yet the song seemed hauntingly familiar.

The song was the song of rice. It sang of the sowing of the unhusked seed rice, and of the careful transplanting of the seedling from seedbed to the newly ploughed fields. It sang of the months of weeding, of watering, of waiting as the stalks grew tall and green, then ripened into a dry brown. It sang of the days spent harvesting and threshing, milling and winnowing the grain, for a single ricebowl to be filled.

The melody and the words rippled outwards, filling the cool night air, until the last note died away, sharp and sweet.

Jinda sat absolutely still. No, she had heard nothing like this before, and yet she felt as if she had known the song all her life. How could this be?

Mingfong Ho

TO KILL A MOCKINGBIRD

The feeling grew until the atmosphere in the courtroom was exactly the same as a cold February morning, when the mocking-birds were still, and the carpenters had stopped hammering on Miss Maudie's new house, and every wood door in the neighborhood was shut as tight as the doors of the Radley Place. A deserted, waiting, empty street, and the courtroom was packed with people. A steaming summer night was no different from a winter morning. Mr Heck Tate, who had entered the courtroom and was talking to Atticus, might have been wearing his high boots and lumber jacket. Atticus had stopped his tranquil journey and had put his foot onto the bottom rung of a chair; as he listened to what Mr Tate was saying, he ran his hand slowly up and down his thigh. I expected Mr Tate to say any minute, "Take him, Mr Finch..."

But Mr Tate said, "This court will come to order," in a voice that rang with authority, and the heads below us jerked up. Mr. Tate left the room and returned with Tom Robinson. He steered Tom to his place beside Atticus, and stood there. Judge Taylor had roused himself to sudden alertness and was sitting up straight, looking at the empty jury box.

What happened after that had a dreamlike quality; in a dream I saw the jury return, moving like underwater swimmers, and Judge Taylor's voice came from far away, and was tiny. I saw something only a lawyer's child could be expected to see, could be expected to watch for, and it was like watching Atticus walk into the street, raise a rifle to his shoulder and pull the trigger, but watching all the time knowing that the gun was empty.

A jury never looks at a defendant it has convicted, and when this jury came in, not one of them looked at Tom Robinson. The foreman handed a piece of paper to Mr Tate who handed it to the clerk who handed it to the judge...

I shut my eyes. Judge Taylor was polling the jury: "Guilty... guilty... guilty ... guilty..."

Harper Lee

THE LAKE AT THE END OF THE WORLD

I remember a time long ago, years before Dad's accident, when Mum was in tears and Dad was trying to comfort her much as I am now. It was different then because Mum wasn't broken and defeated. She was in a rage. 'How much longer?' she was shouting. 'How much longer do I have to put up with this? Stuck here in the bush by a duckpond - no television, no newspapers, no one to talk to, no new books, five minutes each night talking to people stuck in some other bit of godforsaken bush with nothing more to tell me than how many carrots they've bloody planted - ' Dad was able to comfort her as I am not because he missed all those things too. I was six or seven then, and I said 'Tell me about television and newspapers', because I knew there'd be wonderful stories for me as they almost fell over themselves telling me about things they'd seen on television, old movies, plays, series, news stories about disasters and political scandals written in the newspapers and shown on television almost as soon as they happened. Then there'd be the stories about the lake and the people who used to live here. And they'd be laughing and happy again and talking to each other more than to me. They'd open one of the precious bottles of wine to drink and I would be given a tiny drop mixed with water and it would be pink and sour and lovely - now I realise that this sequence of events occurred perhaps many times while I was little. After I was nine or ten, nobody talked about newspapers or television any more. I still read about them from time to time in the books that are stacked around the house, as well as reading about train journeys and holidays at the beach and people falling in love and kids going to school and lots of other things that don't happen any more.

Caroline Macdonald

GHOST SONG

The stranger stood still, watching Malyuta come, and grinning.

The stranger had a thin, wrinkled face that peered from a thick growth of grey-streaked black hair and beard. His grin showed large white teeth, and crinkled his face into many fine lines. Despite the midsummer heat, he was dressed for winter, as if he had come, in a moment, from the far north where it was still cold. Around his shoulders, in heavy, soft, rank folds, hung the yellow-white skin of a white bear. Its head hung upside-down on the man's shoulders. Its paws, with long black claws, dangled at his sides. Underneath the bearskin cloak the man wore trousers and tunic of reindeer hide, decorated with bones, beads, feathers and brass-rings; and so fantastically embroidered that Malyuta's tired eyes were confused by the many intertwining patterns. On the man's feet were embroidered Lappish boots, and big Lappish mittens were on his hands. A shaman, a night-coming witch - for however brightly the sun shone outside, it was night, white midnight, the last hour of Midsummer's Day.

'I have come for my child,' said the stranger.

'What child?' Malyuta asked, though he both knew and dreaded the answer.

The witch turned towards the bed where Yefrosinia slept, his heavy boots padding softly on the floor like a bear's paws. But Malyuta, with a jump, reached the bed first and took the baby up in his own arms.

'*My* son,' he said. '*My* child.'

Susan Price

I CAPTURE THE CASTLE

Simon stamped out the dying embers while I went up to close the door of the tower. I stood at the top of the steps for a moment, trying to capture the feelings I usually have on Midsummer Eve - for I had been too occupied in entertaining Simon to think about them before. And suddenly I knew that I had been right in fearing this might be my last year for the rites - that if I ever held them again *I* should be "playing with the children". I only felt the smallest pang of sadness, because the glory of supper at Scoatney was stretching ahead of me; but I said to myself that, Simon or no Simon, I was going to give the farewell call - a farewell for ever this time, not just for a year. The call is a queer wordless cry made up of all the vowel sounds - it was thrilling when Rose and I used to make it together, but I do it fairly well by myself. "Ayieou!" I called - and it echoed back from the castle walls as I knew it would. Then Helod'se raised her head and howled - and that echoed, too. Simon was fascinated; he said it was the best moment of the rites.

Walking down Belmotte was the oddest sensation - every step took us deeper into the mist until at last it closed over our heads. It was like being drowned in the ghost of water.

Dodie Smith

GRADE EIGHT

THE HILL

Breathless, we flung us on the windy hill,
Laughed in the sun, and kissed the lovely grass.
You said, 'Through glory and ecstasy we pass;
Wind, sun, and earth remain, the birds sing still,
When we are old, are old...' 'And when we die
All's over that is ours; and life burns on
Through other lovers, other lips,' said I,
'Heart of my heart, our heaven is now, is won!'

'We are Earth's best, that learnt her lesson here.
Life is our cry. We have kept the Faith!' we said;
'We shall go down with unreluctant tread
Rose-crowned into the darkness!'... Proud we were,
And laughed, that had such brave true things to say.
- And then you suddenly cried, and turned away.

Rupert Brooke

SONNET 138

When my love swears that she is made of truth,
I do believe her, though I know she lies,
That she might think me some untutored youth,
Unlearned in the world's false subtleties.
Thus vainly thinking that she thinks me young,
Although she knows my days are past the best,
Simply I credit her false-speaking tongue:
On both sides thus is simple truth suppressed.
But wherefore says she not she is unjust?
And wherefore say not I that I am old?
O, love's best habit is in seeming trust,
And age in love loves not to have years told.
    Therefore I lie with her and she with me,
    And in our faults by lies we flattered be.

William Shakespeare

'the Cambridge ladies'

the Cambridge ladies who live in furnished souls
are unbeautiful and have comfortable minds
(also, with the church's protestant blessings
daughters, unscented shapeless spirited)
they believe in Christ and Longfellow, both dead,
are invariably interested in so many things -
at the present writing one still finds
delighted fingers knitting for the is it Poles?
perhaps. While permanent faces coyly bandy
scandal of Mrs N and Professor D
. . . . the Cambridge ladies do not care, above
Cambridge if sometimes in its box of
sky lavender and cornerless, the
moon rattles like a fragment of angry candy

e.e. cummings

IF YOU WANT TO KNOW ME

If you want to know me
examine with careful eyes
this bit of black wood
which some unknown Makonde[*] brother
cut and carved
with his inspired hands
in the distant lands of the North.

This is what I am
empty sockets despairing of possessing life
a mouth torn open in an anguished wound
huge hands outspread
and raised in imprecation and in threat

---

* The Makonde, who live in Northern Mozambique and Southern Tanzania, are famed
for their strange and expressionistic wood sculpture

a body tattooed with wounds seen and unseen
from the harsh whipstrokes of slavery
tortured and magnificent
proud and mysterious
Africa from head to foot
this is what I am.

Noemia de Sousa

A SLICE OF WEDDING CAKE

Why have such scores of lovely, gifted girls
    Married impossible men?
Simple self-sacrifice may be ruled out,
    And missionary endeavour, nine times out of ten.

Repeat 'impossible men': not merely rustic,
    Foul-tempered or depraved
(Dramatic foils chosen to show the world
    How well women behave, and always have behaved).

Impossible men: idle, illiterate,
    Self-pitying, dirty, sly,
For whose appearance even in City parks
    Excuses must be made to casual passers-by.

Has God's supply of tolerable husbands
    Fallen, in fact, so low?
Or do I always over-value woman
    At the expense of man?
           Do I?
           It might be so.

Robert Graves

TONIGHT AT NOON[*]

(for Charlie Mingus and the Clayton Squares)

Tonight at noon
Supermarkets will advertise 3d EXTRA on everything
Tonight at noon
Children from happy families will be sent to live in a home
Elephants will tell each other human jokes
America will declare peace on Russia
World War I generals will sell poppies in the streets on
    November 11th
The first daffodils of autumn will appear
When the leaves fall upwards to the trees

Tonight at noon
Pigeons will hunt cats through city backyards
Hitler will tell us to fight on the beaches and on the landing
    fields
A tunnel full of water will be built under Liverpool
Pigs will be sighted flying in formation over Woolton
and Nelson will not only get his eye back but his arm as well
White Americans will demonstrate for equal rights in front of
    the Black House
and the Monster has just created Dr Frankenstein

Girls in bikinis are moonbathing
Folksongs are being sung by real folk
Art galleries are closed to people over 21
Poets get their poems in the Top 20
Politicians are elected to insane asylums
There's jobs for everyone and nobody wants them
In back alleys everywhere teenage-lovers are kissing in broad
    daylight.

---

* The title of this poem is taken from an LP by Charlie Mingus, *Tonight At Noon*

In forgotten graveyards the dead will quietly bury the living
and
You will tell me you love me
Tonight at noon.

Adrian Henri

ALONE

From childhood's hour I have not been
As others were - I have not seen
As others saw - I could not bring
My passions from a common spring.
From the same source I have not taken
My sorrow; I could not awaken
My heart to joy at the same tone;
And all I lov'd, *I* lov'd alone.
Then - in my childhood - in the dawn
Of a most stormy life - was drawn
From every depth of good and ill
The mystery which binds me still:
From the torrent, or the fountain,
From the red cliff of the mountain,
From the sun that 'round me roll'd
In its autumn tint of gold -
From the lightning in the sky
As it pass'd me flying by -
From the thunder and the storm,
And the cloud that took the form
(When the rest of Heaven was blue)
Of a demon in my view.

Edgar Allan Poe

THE LAKE ISLE OF INNISFREE

I will arise and go now, and go to Innisfree,
And a small cabin build there, of clay and wattles made:
Nine bean-rows will I have there, a hive for the honey-bee
And live alone in the bee-loud glade.

And I shall have some peace there, for peace comes dropping slow,
Dropping from the veils of the morning to where the cricket sings;
There midnight's all a glimmer, and noon a purple glow,
And evening full of the linnet's wings.

I will arise and go now, for always night and day
I hear lake water lapping with low sounds by the shore;
While I stand on the roadway, or on the pavements grey,
I hear it in the deep heart's core.

W.B. Yeats

VILLETTE

I suppose people who go every night to places of public amusement, can hardly enter into the fresh gala feeling with which an opera or a concert is enjoyed by those for whom it is a rarity. I am not sure that I expected great pleasure from the concert, having but a very vague notion of its nature, but I liked the drive there well. The snug comfort of the close carriage on a cold though fine night, the pleasure of setting out with companions so cheerful and friendly, the sight of the stars glinting fitfully through the trees as we rolled along the avenue; then the freer burst of the night-sky when we issued forth to the open chaussée, the passage through the city gates, the lights there burning, the guards there posted, the pretence of inspection to which we there submitted, and which amused us so much - all these small matters had for me, in their novelty, a peculiarly exhilarating charm. How much of it lay in the atmosphere of friendship diffused about me, I know not: Dr John and his mother were both in their finest mood, contending animatedly with each other the whole way, and as frankly kind to me as if I had been of their kin.

Our way lay through some of the best streets of Villette, streets brightly lit, and far more lively now than at high noon. How brilliant seemed the shops! How glad, gay, and abundant flowed the tide of life along the broad pavement! While I looked, the thought of the Rue Fossette came across me - of the walled-in garden and the school-house, and of the dark, vast 'classes', where, as at this very hour, it was my wont to wander all solitary, gazing at the stars through the high, blindless windows, and listening to the distant voice of the reader in the refectory, monotonously exercised upon the 'lecture pieuse'. Thus must I soon again listen and wander; and this shadow of the future stole with timely sobriety across the radiant present.

Charlotte Bronte

I'M THE KING OF THE CASTLE

When he first saw the crow, he took no notice. There had been several crows. This one glided down into the corn on its enormous, ragged black wings. He began to be aware of it when it rose up suddenly, circled overhead, and then dived, to land not very far away from him. Kingshaw could see the feathers on its head, shining blank in between the butter-coloured cornstalks. Then it rose, and circled, and came down again, this time not quite landing, but flapping about his head, beating its wings and making a sound like flat leather pieces being slapped together. It was the largest crow he had ever seen. As it came down for the third time, he looked up and noticed its beak, opening in a screech. The inside of its mouth was scarlet, it had small glinting eyes.

Kingshaw got up and flapped his arms. For a moment, the bird retreated a little way off, and higher up in the sky. He began to walk rather quickly back, through the path in the corn, looking ahead of him. Stupid to be scared of a rotten bird. What could a bird do? But he felt his own extreme isolation, high up in the cornfield.

For a moment, he could only hear the soft thudding of his own footsteps, and the silky sound of the corn, brushing against him. Then, there was a rush of air, as the great crow came beating down, and wheeled about his head. The beak opened and the hoarse caaw came out again and again, from inside the scarlet mouth.

Kingshaw began to run...

Susan Hill

MR NORRIS CHANGES TRAINS

An hour later, Arthur returned home. I followed him into his room to break the news.

'Schmidt's been here.'

If Arthur's wig had been suddenly jerked from his head by a fisherman, he could hardly have looked more startled.

'William, please tell me the worst at once. Don't keep me in suspense. What time was this? Did you see him yourself? What did he say?'

'He's trying to blackmail you, isn't he?'

Arthur looked at me quickly.

'Did he admit that?'

'He as good as told me. He says he's written to you already, and that if you don't do what he wants by the end of the week there'll be trouble.'

'He actually said that? Oh dear...'

'You should have told me he'd written,' I said reproachfully.

'I know, dear boy, I know...' Arthur was the picture of distress. 'It's been on the tip of my tongue several times this last fortnight. But I didn't want to worry you unnecessarily. I kept hoping that, somehow, it might all blow over.'

'Now look here, Arthur; the point is this: does Schmidt really know anything about you which can do you harm?'

He had been nervously pacing the room, and now sank, a disconsolate shirt-sleeved figure, into a chair, forlornly regarding his button-boots.

'Yes, William.' His voice was small and apologetic. 'I'm afraid he does.'

Christopher Isherwood

SONS AND LOVERS

Paul was now fourteen, and was looking for work. He was a rather small and rather finely-made boy, with dark brown hair and light blue eyes. His face had already lost its youthful chubbiness, and was becoming something like William's - rough-featured, almost rugged - and it was extraordinarily mobile. Usually he looked as if he saw things, was full of life, and warm; then his smile, like his mother's, came suddenly and was very lovable; and then, when there was any clog in his soul's quick running, his face went stupid and ugly. He was the sort of boy that becomes a clown and a lout as soon as he is not understood, or feels himself held cheap; and, again, is adorable at the first touch of warmth.

He suffered very much from the first contact with anything. When he was seven, the starting school had been a nightmare and a torture to him. But afterwards he liked it. And now that he felt he had to go out into life, he went through agonies of shrinking self-consciousness. He was quite a clever painter for a boy of his years, and he knew some French and German and mathematics that Mr Heaton had taught him. But nothing he had was of any commercial value. He was not strong enough for heavy manual work, his mother said. He did not care for making things with his hands, preferred racing about or making excursions into the country, or reading, or painting.

'What do you want to be?' his mother asked.

'Anything.'

'That is no answer,' said Mrs Morel.

But it was quite truthfully the only answer he could give. His ambition, as far as this world's gear went, was quietly to earn his thirty or thirty-five shillings a week somewhere near home, and then, when his father died, have a cottage with his mother, paint and go out as he liked, and live happy ever after.

D.H. Lawrence

THE TREE OF HANDS

What happened next made Benet glad Jason wasn't in the room to see it. Though he must have heard Mopsa's screams, he wasn't present. Mopsa simply opened her mouth as wide as it would go and let out screams of terrific volume. She stood there screaming into Benet's face. Benet had never seen or heard anything like it and for a moment, beyond putting her hands up ineffectually to cover her ears, she couldn't move. She knew the prescribed thing was to strike a hysterical person in the face but she couldn't bring herself to do this; her arm felt as weak as when one attempts to strike a blow in a dream.

'Mother, stop. Please stop... '

Mopsa went on screaming. She fell on her knees and put her arms round Benet's legs, hugging her legs and screaming, breathily and hoarsely now as she exhausted herself. She crouched on the floor, scrabbling at Benet's shoes.

'Mother, I can't stand this. Please stop.'

For a moment she had been afraid. The skin on the back of her neck had crept and she had felt the hairs standing erect on gooseflesh. She had been frightened of pathetic, crazed Mopsa. She bent down and got hold of Mopsa's shoulders and shook her, though without much result. Mopsa slithered out of her grasp and drummed her fists on the floor and shouted: 'They'll commit me, they'll make you commit me, I'll be certified, I'll never come out, I'll die in there!'

Ruth Rendell

WIDE SARGASSO SEA

One morning when I woke I ached all over. Not the cold, another sort of ache. I saw that my wrists were red and swollen. Grace said, 'I suppose you're going to tell me that you don't remember anything about last night.'

'When was last night?' I said.

'Yesterday.'

'I don't remember yesterday.'

'Last night a gentleman came to see you,' she said.

'Which of them was that?'

Because I knew that there were strange people in the house. When I took the keys and went into the passage I heard them laughing and talking in the distance, like birds, and there were lights on the floor beneath.

Turning a corner I saw a girl coming out of her bedroom. She wore a white dress and she was humming to herself. I flattened myself against the wall for I did not wish her to see me, but she stopped and looked round. She saw nothing but shadows, I took care of that, but she didn't walk to the head of the stairs. She ran. She met another girl and the second girl said, 'Have you seen a ghost?' - 'I didn't see anything but I thought I felt something.' - 'That is the ghost,' the second one said and they went down the stairs together.

'Which of these people came to see me, Grace Poole?' I said.

He didn't come. Even if I was asleep I would have known. He hasn't come yet.

Jean Rhys

TONO-BUNGAY

'What is Tono-Bungay?' I asked.

My uncle hesitated. 'Tell you after lunch, George,' he said. 'Come along!' and having locked up the sanctum after himself, led the way along a narrow, dirty pavement, lined with barrows and swept at times by avalanche-like porters bearing burthens to vans, to Farringdon Street. He hailed a passing cab superbly, and the cabman was infinitely respectful. 'Schäfers's,' he said, and off we went side by side - and with me more and more amazed at all these things - to Schäfers's Hotel, the second of the two big

places with huge, lace-curtain-covered windows, near the corner
of Blackfriars Bridge.

I will confess I felt a magic change in our relative proportions
as the two colossal, pale-blue-and-red liveried porters of
Schäfers's held open the inner doors for us with a respectful
salutation that in some manner they seemed to confine wholly
to my uncle. Instead of being about four inches taller, I felt at
least the same size as he, and very much slenderer. Still more
respectful waiters relieved him of the new hat and the dignified
umbrella, and took his orders for our lunch. He gave them with
a fine assurance.

He nodded to several of the waiters.

'They know me, George, already,' he said. 'Point me out.
Live place! Eye for coming men!'

The detailed business of the lunch engaged our attention for
a while, and then I leant across my plate. 'And *now*?' said I.

'It's the secret of vigour. Didn't you read that label?'

'Yes, but - '

'It's selling like hot cakes.'

'And what is it?' I pressed.

'Well,' said my uncle, and then leant forward and spoke softly
under cover of his hand, 'It's nothing more or less than ...'

H.G. Wells

FROST IN MAY

But at thirteen, Nanda had not entirely decided where her
talents lay. When the novel, scribbled in bed by the dim light of
a low burning gas-jet outside her cubicle, went badly, as it
usually did, she would turn to playwriting, only to realise, as the
second act petered out half-way through, that she would never
write anything half as good as Léonie's *Death of Socrates*. Often
she thought she would like to be a painter, and, encouraged by
Clare, who drew remarkably well, she would turn out weak little

landscapes of flat country with two or three poplar trees grouped against acres of sky. However, the ultramarine in her paint-box gave out so early in each term that she usually fell back on music. Apart from the regular hour each day, she would spend her free study in the piano cells, playing Chopin's nocturnes with tremendous expression and more pedal than accuracy. But the sight of Léonie making appalling faces at her through the window had severely shaken her confidence and lately her musical activities had taken the form of listening admiringly while Léo drummed out Bach fugues with great sternness and precision. In the background, of course, there was acting. At Lippington, as at most convent schools, there were plays and tableaux and dramatic recitations every term, and after a small success as an English Martyr or Prince Arthur or Alice in Wonderland, Nanda was usually ready to abandon all her other pursuits for the stage.

Antonia White

BRONZE MEDAL

FOR THE FALLEN

September 1914

With proud thanksgiving, a mother for her children,
England mourns for her dead across the sea.
Flesh of her flesh they were, spirit of her spirit,
Fallen in the cause of the free.

Solemn the drums thrill: Death august and royal
Sings sorrow up into immortal spheres.
There is music in the midst of desolation
And a glory that shines upon our tears.

They went with songs to the battle, they were young,
Straight of limb, true of eye, steady and aglow.
They were staunch to the end against odds uncounted,
They fell with their faces to the foe.

They shall grow not old, as we that are left grow old:
Age shall not weary them, nor the years condemn,
At the going down of the sun and in the morning
We will remember them.

They mingle not with their laughing comrades again,
They sit no more at familiar tables of home;
They have no lot in our labour of the day-time;
They sleep beyond England's foam.

But where our desires are and our hopes profound,
Felt as a well-spring that is hidden from sight,
To the innermost heart of their own land they are known
As the stars are known to the Night;

As the stars that shall be bright when we are dust,
Moving in marches upon the heavenly plain,
As the stars that are starry in the time of our darkness,
To the end, to the end, they remain.

Laurence Binyon

THE HE-BEAR'S LAMENT

after Pushkin

O listen! Listen!
The he-bear is roaring, high up in the valley,
His voice is trembling
The young green leaves that shiver and dance
On the birch-tree tips.

O listen! Listen!
The hunter has killed the brave brown she-bear,
The hunter has taken the three round
Bear-cubs, the bouncing bear-cubs,
And bundled them into his hunter's bag.

The hunter has speared
The she-bear's white belly, he killed her
And skinned her, and left her for crow-meat.
He rolled up the beautiful she-bear's pelt
And has taken it home to his wife for a coat.

And listen! O listen!
The he-bear is pounding the earth with his paws,
As he calls for his mate, who played
In the river, who romped there together
With him on the banks of their summer lair.

The wailing has shuddered
The roots of the forest: the silence is hollow -
It rings with the echo. The deer turn to statues
And even the wolf lifts his head and is still
As his nose takes the scent of blood on the air.

And all the small creatures
Of the peaceable kingdom begin to gather
To hear the bear's mourning:
The flat-tailed beaver, the weasel, the squirrel;
The stoat with his tumbling clown-like dance.

They run to be there to share
In his grieving, to sit in a circle of sorrow
About him, the Lord of the Woods, the great he-bear.
The marmot, the pious tawny hedgehog,
And a limping, lop-eared, haunted hare.

Stuart Henson

SONNET

*At the moment, if you're seen reading
poetry in a train, the carriage empties instantly.*

*Andrew Motion
(Guardian interview)*

Indeed 'tis true. I travel here and there
On British Rail a lot. I've often said
That if you haven't got the first-class fare
You really need a book of verse instead.
Then, should you find that all the seats are taken,
Brandish your Edward Thomas, Yeats or Pound.
Your fellow-passengers, severely shaken,
Will almost all be loath to stick around.
Recent research in railway sociology
Shows it's best to read the stuff aloud:
A few choice bits from Motion's new anthology
And you'll be lonelier than any cloud.
This stratagem's a godsend to recluses
And demonstrates that poetry has its uses.

Wendy Cope

LOVE

Love bade me welcome; yet my soul drew back,
       Guilty of dust and sin.
But quick-eyed Love, observing me grow slack
       From my first entrance in,
Drew nearer to me, sweetly questioning,
       If I lacked anything.

'A guest', I answered, 'worthy to be here.'
       Love said, 'You shall be he.'
'I, the unkind, ungrateful? Ah, my dear,
       I cannot look on thee.'
Love took my hand, and smiling did reply,
       'Who made the eyes but I?'

'Truth, Lord, but I have marred them; let my shame
       Go where it doth deserve.'
'And know you not', says Love, 'who bore the blame?'
       'My dear, then I will serve.'
'You must sit down', says Love, 'and taste my meat.'
       So I did sit and eat.

George Herbert

YOUNG WOMAN

Young Woman, fragile shoot
I am afraid for you
You are so vulnerable.

Young Woman, Tender vine
I am afraid for you
You are denied guidance.

Young Woman, slender leafy plant
I am afraid for you
You are so innocent
Glorying the discovery
Of your beauty.

Young Woman, blossoming palm-tree
You are on the threshold
Of life in all its fullness
I am afraid for you
You are exposed to the elements
Of violence, disillusionment
and discrimination,
Fruits of an unjust social and
economic arrangement.

Young Woman
Be a sealed fountain
in an enclosed garden
Whose walls are to be scaled
When you are Woman, Conscious, Positive,
Goal setting, Confident Woman.

Young Woman, be wise
Guard your dignity
Acknowledge your potential.

Father, Mother, Older Man, Older Woman,
Uncle, Aunt, Brother, Sister, Young Woman,
Be a hedge around her
Bruise not the flower.

Nelcia Robinson

SHE IS

She is...
She is...
    A blanket - stifling and constricting - a blanket whose security
    I love yet hate - a blanket which holds me too close - too warm.
She is...
She is...
    a tornado - ripping apart my foundations
    and crushing me into miniscule bits of shame...
    yet after the
    tornado comes the rain of her tears, my tears...
    mingling till
    we forget our sorrow and laugh
        once again.
She is...
She is...
    a cat. A black panther, sleek and beautiful -
              A tiger.. waiting for its prey...
           A kitten playing with a ball of wool...
             a lioness, majestic and aloof.
She is...
    a guardian, a friend, a confidante,
    an enemy, one loved with a love as strong as her own will.
    She is good yet bad ... black yet white ... happy yet sad..
    ..a kaleidoscope of emotions and colours and moods.
She is...
    My mother.

Leone Ross

NOR WE OF HER TO HIM

He said no word of her to us
Nor we of her to him,
But oh it saddenend us to see
How wan he grew and thin.
We said: She eats him day and night
And draws the blood from him,
We did not know but said we thought
This was why he grew thin.

One day we called and rang the bell,
No answer came within,
We said: she must have took him off
To the forest old and grim,
It has fell out, we said, that she
Eats him in forest grim,
And how can we help him being eaten
Up in forests grim?

It is a restless time we spend,
We have no help for him,
We walk about and go to bed,
It is no help to him.
Sometimes we shake our heads and say
It might have better been
If he had spoke to us of her
Or we of her to him.
Which makes us feel helpful, until
The silence comes again.

Stevie Smith

ON GILES AND JOAN

Who says that Giles and Joan at discord be?
The observing neighbours no such mood can see.
Indeed, poor Giles repents he married ever.
But that his Joan doth too. And Giles would never,
By his free will, be in Joan's company.
No more would Joan he should. Giles riseth early,
And having got him out of doors is glad.
The like is Joan. But turning home, is sad.
And so is Joan. Oft-times, when Giles doth find
Harsh sights at home, Giles wisheth he were blind.
All this doth Joan. Or that his long-yarned life
Were quite out-spun. The like wish hath his wife.
The children, that he keeps, Giles swears are none
Of his begetting. And so swears his Joan.
In all affections she concurreth still.
If, now, with man and wife, to will, and nill
The selfsame things, a note of concord be:
I know no couple better can agree!

Ben Jonson

THE WAY OF WYRD

I was getting shakily to my feet when Wulf bounded to my side. He put an arm around my waist and led me slowly back into the clearing.

'You are doing well, Brand,' he said excitedly. 'But you lost concentration. You must keep your whole being focused on the fibres - keep them in your vision all the time. This is no task for a mind that flickers like a candle.'

Wulf drew me to the back of the clearing, pointed towards the fire and then ruffled my hair playfully.

'Right over the fires into the trees!' he chuckled.

I closed my eyes.

This time I had waited only a short time when I suddenly staggered forward, sucked by a swirling wind that cut cold across my stomach; then I ran towards the nearest fire with long, bouncing steps. Just before I reached the fire a fibre appeared before me like an incandescent rope reaching from my body into the sky, and I rose effortlessly from the ground. As I plunged through the smoke I thought I glimpsed at eye level the high branches of surrounding trees, then I hit the ground at tremendous speed. This time I absorbed the shock by bending my legs on impact. When I looked around in the darkness, I realised that I was sitting in a small patch of fern, by the edge of the clearing and at least ten paces from the second fire.

Wulf ran up and pulled me to my feet. His expression was all the encouragement I needed: I knew that I was now jumping with my fibres.

Brian Bates

A PARTICULAR FRIENDSHIP

There is a little owl somewhere. I hear him too on crisp nights, but haven't as yet found his nest. I rather think it's in one of the dead elms down by the old tennis courts. Did you make those? Did you play there often? Forlorn now and abandoned. The wire rusts and sags, torn in great holes, the courts scabbed with tufts of fireweed, ragwort and clumps of glossy nettles which attract the Admirals and Peacocks, the lead markings buckled and twisted with the frosts and suns of seasons. Bracken and bramble proliferate, hip high, and the tall row of Lombardy poplars on the east boundary are as high as steeples, some are dead, but there are three like Proust's at Martinville ... two quite near, the third a little further off ... they seem to change places as one walks down through the high rutted banks of the chestnut walk to the ponds. There is nothing I can do now to wrest them back from their wilderness. The courts I mean. Left too long... since, I suppose, you went. There is a wistful, melancholic atmosphere especially on long summer evenings when the shadows lengthen and the sun begins to slip down behind the trees. I imagine the ghosts of players long past. Not necessarily because they are dead! I suppose I really mean The Shades. The transparency we must leave behind us wherever we have been ... do you know what I mean? Probably not. I am a bad explainer. But on still summer evenings I imagine the 'shades' of players there, long forgotten. But not you ... for you are remembered now!

Dirk Bogarde

THE MOONSTONE

Luncheon over, my aunt said: 'Remember what the doctor told you, Rachel, about quieting yourself with a book after taking your meals.'

'I'll go into the library, mamma,' she answered. 'But if Godfrey calls, mind I am told of it. I am dying for more news of him, after his adventure in Northumberland Street.' She kissed her mother on the forehead, and looked my way. 'Good-bye, Clack,' she said, carelessly. Her insolence roused no angry feeling in me; I only made a private memorandum to pray for her.

When we were left by ourselves, my aunt told me the whole horrible story of the Indian Diamond, which, I am happy to know, it is not necessary to repeat here. She did not conceal from me that she would have preferred keeping silence on the subject. But when her own servants all knew of the loss of the Moonstone, and when some of the circumstances had actually found their way into the newspapers - when strangers were speculating whether there was any connection between what had happened at Lady Verinder's country house and what had happened in Northumberland Street and Alfred Place - concealment was not to be thought of, and perfect frankness became a necessity as well as a virtue.

Wilkie Collins

DAISY MILLER

Winterbourne perceived at some distance a little man standing with folded arms nursing his cane. He had a handsome face, an artfully poised hat, a glass in one eye, and a nosegay in his buttonhole. Winterbourne looked at him a moment and then said, "Do you mean to speak to that man?"

"Do I mean to speak to him? Why, you don't suppose I mean to communicate by signs?"

"Pray understand, then," said Winterbourne, "that I intend to remain with you."

Daisy stopped and looked at him, without a sign of troubled consciousness in her face, with nothing but the presence of her charming eyes and her happy dimples. "Well, she's a cool one!" thought the young man.

"I don't like the way you say that," said Daisy. "It's too imperious."

"I beg your pardon if I say it wrong. The main point is to give you an idea of my meaning."

The young girl looked at him more gravely, but with eyes that were prettier than ever. "I have never allowed a gentleman to dictate to me, or to interfere with anything I do."

"I think you have made a mistake," said Winterbourne. "You should sometimes listen to a gentleman - the right one!"

Daisy began to laugh again. "I do nothing but listen to gentlemen!" she exclaimed. "Tell me if Mr Giovanelli is the right one?"

The gentleman with the nosegay in his bosom had now perceived our two friends, and was approaching the young girl with obsequious rapidity. He bowed to Winterbourne as well as to the latter's companion; he had a brilliant smile, an intelligent eye; Winterbourne thought him not a bad-looking fellow. But he nevertheless said to Daisy, "No, he's not the right one."

Henry James

MIGUEL STREET

The men in the street didn't like Bhakcu because they considered him a nuisance. But I liked him for the same reason that I liked Popo, the carpenter. For, thinking about it now, Bhakcu was also an artist. He interfered with motor-cars for the joy of the thing, and he never seemed worried about money.

But his wife was worried. She, like my mother, thought that she was born to be a clever handler of money, born to make money sprout from nothing at all.

She talked over the matter with my mother one day.

My mother said, 'Taxi making a lot of money these days, taking Americans and their girl friends all over the place.'

So Mrs Bhakcu made her husband buy a lorry.

This lorry was really the pride of Miguel Street. It was a big new Bedford and we all turned out to welcome it when Bhakcu brought it home for the first time.

Even Hat was impressed. 'If is one thing the English people could build,' he said, 'is a lorry. This is not like your Ford and your Dodge, you know.'

Bhakcu began working on it that very afternoon, and Mrs Bhakcu went around telling people, 'Why not come and see how *he* working on the Bedford?'

From time to time Bhakcu would crawl out from under the lorry and polish the wings and the bonnet. Then he would crawl under the lorry again. But he didn't look happy.

The next day the people who had lent the money to buy the Bedford formed a deputation and came to Bhakcu's house, begging him to desist.

Bhakcu remained under the lorry all the time, refusing to reply. The money-lenders grew angry, and some of the women among them began to cry. Even that failed to move Bhakcu, and in the end the deputation just had to go away.

V.S. Naipaul

A FAR CRY FROM KENSINGTON

One Saturday morning I had gone down to see if there was any post for me. I passed Wanda on the stairs. She was smiling with her letters in her hand. For me, there was a letter from a cousin. I stood beside the hall-stand, opening it. Suddenly, from Wanda's room came a long, loud, high-pitched cry which diminished into a sustained, distant and still audible ululation.

I ran upstairs. Milly came out to see what was the matter and stood on the lower steps, looking up. I knocked on Wanda's door at the moment that a second lament came piercing from inside the room; I wasted no time in going straight in. There was Wanda in her black working jumper and skirt, her blue carpet-slippers, holding a letter in her hand and the long cry issuing from her mouth. Her eyes were terrorized. She handed me the letter. I made her sit down before I read it, imagining it to be news of a sudden death in the family, at least. The letter read:

> Mrs Podolak,
> We, the Organisers, have our eyes on you. You are conducting a dressmaking business but you are not declaring your income to the Authorities.
> Take care.
>   An Organiser.

The envelope was cheap brown manilla. It had been posted at Westminster.

'Mrs Hawkins,' said Wanda, 'this is the end of me. They will put me in prison. They will deport me.'

Muriel Spark

THE PEARL

Juana steadied the boat while he climbed in. His eyes were shining with excitement, but in decency he pulled up his rock, and then he pulled up his basket of oysters and lifted them in. Juana sensed his excitement, and she pretended to look away. It is not good to want a thing too much. It sometimes drives the luck away. You must want it just enough, and you must be very tactful with God or the gods. But Juana stopped breathing. Very deliberately Kino opened his short strong knife. He looked speculatively at the basket. Perhaps it would be better to open *the* oyster last. He took a small oyster from the basket, cut the muscle, searched the folds of flesh, and threw it in the water. Then he seemed to see the great oyster for the first time. He squatted in the bottom of the canoe, picked up the shell and examined it. The flutes were shining black to brown, and only a few small barnacles adhered to the shell. Now Kino was reluctant to open it. What he had seen, he knew, might be a reflection, a piece of flat shell accidentally drifted in or a complete illusion. In this Gulf of uncertain light there were more illusions than realities.

But Juana's eyes were on him and she could not wait. She put her hand on Coyotito's covered head. 'Open it,' she said softly.

Kino deftly slipped his knife into the edge of the shell. Through the knife he could feel the muscle tighten hard. He worked the blade lever-wise and the closing muscle parted and the shell fell apart. The lip-like flesh writhed up and then subsided. Kino lifted the flesh, and there it lay, the great pearl, perfect as the moon. It captured the light and refined it and gave it back in silver incandescence. It was as large as a seagull's egg. It was the greatest pearl in the world.

John Steinbeck

SIR HARRY HOTSPUR OF HUMBLETHWAITE

Poor Lady Elizabeth had not a chance with Cousin George. She succumbed to him at once, not knowing why, but feeling that she herself became bright, amusing, and happy when talking to him. She was a woman not given to familiarities; but she did become familiar with him, allowing him little liberties of expression which no other man would take with her, and putting them all down to the score of cousinhood. He might be a black sheep. She feared there could be but little doubt that he was one. But, from her worsted-work up to the demerits of her dearest friend, he did know how to talk better than any other young man she knew. To Emily, on that first evening, he said very little. When he first met her, he had pressed her hand, and looked into her eyes, and smiled on her with a smile so sweet it was as though a god had smiled on her. She had made up her mind that he should be nothing to her, - nothing beyond a dear cousin; nevertheless, her eye had watched him during the whole hour of dinner, and, not knowing that it was so, she had waited for his coming to them in the evening. Heavens and earth! what an oaf was that young Thoresby as the two stood together near the door! She did not want her cousin to come and talk to her, but she listened and laughed within herself as she saw how pleased was her mother by the attentions of the black sheep.

One word Cousin George did say to Emily Hotspur that night, just as the ladies were leaving the room. It was said in a whisper, with a little laugh, with that air of half joke half earnest which may be so efficacious in conversation: 'I did not go to Goodwood, after all.'

She raised her eyes to his for a quarter of a second, thanking him for his goodness in refraining. 'I don't believe that he is really a black sheep at all,' she said to herself that night, as she laid her head upon her pillow.

Anthony Trollope

SILVER MEDAL

"NASARAYABA"

*("Nasarayaba" means "I rise again" in Garifuna or Black
Carib, the language of the narrator)*

I am an old woman now.
I carry dead dry wood,
On my greying head,
As I walk in the cool morning dew
From farm.
Wood for the fire
Wood to burn
Heavy dead weight,
Like my bones.

When I was young, I walked
Like the young girls, proudly.
The bundle then
Was a baby nestled
In my plump arms.
A bright black-eyed pickney
Tiny mouth sucking at my breast.
Drinking greedily from
My (then) green bones.
Oh, to be young again,
To feel that live weight (so light)
Lifting me into my life
Rather than this heavy
Dead load on my head
That pounds me
Like a hammer
Down into my grave.

But the load
Will be burned
And its heat
Will melt the ice in me.

And I'll rise again
(As I did in my short, hard life)
Triumphant, out of ashes.

Judith Behrendt

WALKING AWAY

It is eighteen years ago, almost to the day -
A sunny day with the leaves just turning,
The touch-lines new-ruled - since I watched you play
Your first game of football, then, like a satellite
Wrenched from its orbit, go drifting away

Behind a scatter of boys. I can see
You walking away from me towards the school
With the pathos of a half-fledged thing set free
Into the wilderness, the gait of one
Who finds no path where the path should be.

That hesitant figure, eddying away
Like a winged seed loosened from its parent stem,
Has something I never quite grasp to convey
About nature's give-and-take - the small, the scorching
Ordeals which fire one's irresolute clay.

I have had worse partings, but none that so
Gnaws at my mind still. Perhaps it is roughly
Saying what God alone could perfectly show -
How selfhood begins with a walking away,
And love is proved in the letting go.

C. Day Lewis

TIANANMEN

Tiananmen
Is broad and clean
And you can't tell
Where the dead have been
And you can't tell
What happened then
And you can't speak
Of Tiananmen.

You must not speak.
You must not think.
You must not dip
Your brush in ink.
You must not say
What happened then,
What happened there
In Tiananmen.

The cruel men
Are old and deaf
Ready to kill
But short of breath
And they will die
Like other men
And they'll lie in state
In Tiananmen.

They lie in state.
They lie in style.
Another lie's
Thrown on the pile,
Thrown on the pile
By the cruel men
To cleanse the blood
From Tiananmen.

Truth is a secret.
Keep it dark.
Keep it dark
In your heart of hearts.
Keep it dark
Till you know when
Truth may return
To Tiananmen.

Tiananmen
Is broad and clean
And you can't tell
Where the dead have been
And you can't tell
When they'll come again.
They'll come again
To Tiananmen.

Hong Kong, 15 June 1989

James Fenton

TRANSLATION

Now that the barbarians have got as far as Picra,
And all the new music is written in the twelve-tone scale,
And I am anyway approaching my fortieth birthday,
        I will dissemble no longer.

I will stop expressing my belief in the rosy
Future of man, and accept the evidence
Of a couple of wretched wars and innumerable
        Abortive revolutions.

I will cease to blame the stupidity of the slaves
Upon their masters and nurture, and will say,
Plainly, that they are enemies to culture,
        Advancement and cleanliness.

SPRING OFFENSIVE

Halted against the shade of a last hill,
They fed, and, lying easy, were at ease
And, finding comfortable chests and knees
Carelessly slept. But many there stood still
To face the stark, blank sky beyond the ridge,
Knowing their feet had come to the end of tͪ

Marvelling they stood, and watched the long grass swirled
By the May breeze, murmurous with wasp and midge,
For though the summer oozed into their veins
Like the injected drug for their bones' pains,
Sharp on their souls hung the imminent line of grass,
Fearfully flashed the sky's mysterious glass.

Hour after hour they ponder the warm field -
And the far valley behind, where the buttercups
Had blessed with gold their slow boots coming up,
Where even the little brambles would not yield,
But clutched and clung to them like sorrowing hands;
They breathe like trees unstirred.

Till like a cold gust thrilled the little word
At which each body and its soul begird
And tighten them for battle. No alarms
Of bugles, no high flags, no clamorous haste -
Only a lift and flare of eyes that faced
The sun, like a friend with whom their love is done.
O larger shone that smile against the sun,
Mightier than his whose bounty these have spurned.

So soon they topped the hill, and raced together
Over an open stretch of herb and heather
Exposed. And instantly the whole sky burned
With fury against them; and soft sudden cups
Opened in thousands for their blood; and the green slopes
Chasmed and steepened sheer to infinite space.

Of them who running on that last high place
Leapt to swift unseen bullets, or went up
On the hot blast and fury of hell's upsurge,
Or plunged and fell away past this world's verge,
Some say God caught them even before they fell.

But what say such as from existence' brink
Ventured but drave too swift to sink,
The few who rushed in the body to enter hell,
And there out-fiending all its fiends and flames
With superhuman inhumanities,
Long-famous glories, immemorial shames -
And crawling slowly back, have by degrees
Regained cool peaceful air in wonder -
Why speak they not of comrades that went under?

Wilfred Owen

FOR A FATHERLESS SON

You will be aware of an absence, presently,
Growing beside you, like a tree,
A death tree, colour gone, an Australian gum tree -
Balding, gelded by lightning an illusion,
And a sky like a pig's backside, an utter lack of attention.

But right now you are dumb.
And I love your stupidity,
The blind mirror of it. I look in
And find no face but my own, and you think that's funny.
It is good for me

To have you grab my nose, a ladder rung.
One day you may touch what's wrong
The small skulls, the smashed blue hills, the godawful hush.
Till then your smiles are found money.

Sylvia Plath

SENSE AND SENSIBILITY

In the evening, as Marianne was discovered to be musical, she was invited to play. The instrument was unlocked, every body prepared to be charmed, and Marianne, who sang very well, at their request went through the chief of the songs which Lady Middleton had brought into the family on her marriage, and which perhaps had lain ever since in the same position on the pianoforte, for her ladyship had celebrated that event by giving up music, although by her mother's account she had played extremely well, and by her own was very fond of it.

Marianne's performance was highly applauded. Sir John was loud in his admiration at the end of every song, and as loud in his conversation with the others while every song lasted. Lady Middleton frequently called him to order, wondered how any one's attention could be diverted from music for a moment, and asked Marianne to sing a particular song which Marianne had just finished. Colonel Brandon alone, of all the party, heard her without being in raptures. He paid her only the compliment of attention; and she felt a respect for him on the occasion, which the others had reasonably forfeited by their shameless want of taste. His pleasure in music, though it amounted not to that extatic delight which alone could sympathize with her own, was estimable when contrasted against the horrible insensibility of the others; and she was reasonable enough to allow that a man of five and thirty might well have outlived all acuteness of feeling and every exquisite power of enjoyment. She was perfectly disposed to make every allowance for the colonel's advanced state of life which humanity required.

Jane Austen

OFF THE RAILS

Memoirs of a train addict

I first discovered trains as a means of truancy, and thus they have remained, irrevocably linked in my mind with the idea of escape. They are the vehicles of romance and adventure, a lifeline promising relief from dullness. I have woven a network of fantasy around the very concept of the train, so wide that the actuality of the journey can rarely outweigh the overall sense of glamour and daring which rail-travel has in my head. Myths begin naturally and then are moulded and sculptured and treasured until they grow out of all proportion to the initial grain of truth. My own love of the railways hovers now somewhere between the improbable and the insane. Sometimes, as I squeeze my way through grime and empty beer cans, past over-stressed commuters or over-wrought shoppers or over-sexed hikers, and the trains are late and the loos blocked and the buffet closed, I stand in wonder at the lengths to which I will go to foster my dream. This dream is of travel and romance, and of romantic travel. I have spent years in seemingly purposeless drifting, but I believe that when I search it is for a moment when time stands still - the pause in the ballet leap, the volatile thrill of perfection. Travelling is like flirting with life. It's like saying 'I would stay and love you, but I have to go; this is my station.' For the rootless and the restless, and the just plain curious, it is a way of being inside the kaleidoscope, but with a way out and a flexible timetable.

Lisa St Aubin de Teràn

COLD COMFORT FARM

"Tes mine?'

'Aye - I mean, yes, it's yours. Your very own. Do take it.'

He took it between his finger and thumb and stood gazing at it. His eyes had filmed over like sightless Atlantic pools before the flurry of the storm breath. His gnarled fingers folded round the handle.

'Aye... 'tes mine,' he muttered. 'Nor house nor kine, and yet 'tes mine ... My little mop!'

He undid the thorn twig which fastened the bosom of his shirt and thrust the mop within. But then he withdrew it again, and replaced the thorn. 'My little mop!' He stood staring at it in a dream.

'Yes. It's to cletter the dishes with,' said Flora, firmly, suddenly foreseeing a new danger on the horizon.

'Nay ... nay,' protested Adam. ''Tes too pretty to cletter those great old dishes wi'. I mun do that with the thorn twigs; they'll serve. I'll keep my little mop in the shed, along wi' our Pointless and our Feckless.'

'They might eat it,' suggested Flora.

'Aye, aye, so they might, Robert Poste's child. Ah, well, I mun hang it up by its liddle red string above the dish-washin' bowl. Niver put my liddle pretty in that gurt old greasy washin'-up water. Aye, 'tes prettier nor apple-blooth, my liddle mop.'

And shuffling across the kitchen, he hung it carefully on the wall above the sink, and stood for some time admiring it. Flora was justifiably irritated, and went crossly out for a walk.

Stella Gibbons

BRIGHTON ROCK

The lights were on in Montpellier Road. Nobody was about, and an empty milk bottle stood outside a gramophone shop; far down were the illuminated clock tower and the public lavatories. The air was fresh like country air. He could imagine he had escaped. He put his hands for warmth into his trouser-pockets and felt a scrap of paper which should not have been there. He drew it out - a scrap torn from a notebook - big, unformed, stranger's writing. He held it up into the grey light and read - with difficulty. 'I love you, Pinkie. I don't care what you do. I love you for ever. You've been good to me. Wherever you go, I'll go too.' She must have written it while he talked to Cubitt and slipped it into his pocket while he slept. He crumpled it in his fist: a dustbin stood outside a fishmonger's - then he held his hand. An obscure sense told him you never knew - it might prove useful one day.

He heard a whisper, looked sharply round, and thrust the paper back. In an alley between two shops, an old woman sat upon the ground; he could just see the rotting and discoloured face: it was like the sight of damnation. Then he heard the whisper, 'Blessed art thou among women,' saw the grey fingers fumbling at the beads. This was not one of the damned; he watched with horrified fascination: this was one of the saved.

Graham Greene

THE FALL OF THE HOUSE OF USHER

The room in which I found myself was very large and lofty. The windows were long, narrow, and pointed, and at so vast a distance from the black oaken floor as to be altogether inaccessible from within. Feeble gleams of encrimsoned light made their way through the trellised panes, and served to render sufficiently distinct the more prominent objects around; the eye, however, struggled in vain to reach the remoter angles of the chamber, or the recesses of the vaulted and fretted ceiling. Dark draperies hung upon the walls. The general furniture was profuse, comfortless, antique, and tattered. Many books and musical instruments lay scattered about, but failed to give any vitality to the scene. I felt that I breathed an atmosphere of sorrow. An air of stern, deep, and irredeemable gloom hung over and pervaded all.

Upon my entrance, Usher arose from a sofa on which he had been lying at full length, and greeted me with a vivacious warmth which had much in it, I at first thought, of an overdone cordiality - of the constrained effort of the *ennuyé* man of the world. A glance, however, at his countenance, convinced me of his perfect sincerity. We sat down; and for some moments, while he spoke not, I gazed upon him with a feeling half of pity, half of awe. Surely, man had never before so terribly altered, in so brief a period, as had Roderick Usher!

Edgar Allan Poe

THE LETTERS OF VINCENT VAN GOGH

Arles, mid October 1888

My dear Theo,

At last I am sending you a small sketch to give you at least an idea of the form which the work is taking. For today I am all right again. My eyes are still tired, but then I had a new idea in my head and here is the sketch of it. Another canvas of size 30. This time it's just simply my bedroom, only here colour is to do everything, and giving by its simplification a grander style to things, is to be suggestive here of *rest* or of sleep in general. In a word, to look at the picture ought to rest the brain or rather the imagination.

The walls are pale violet. The floor is of red tiles.

The wood of the bed and chairs is the yellow of fresh butter, the sheet and pillows very light lemon-green.

The coverlet scarlet. The window green.

The toilet table orange, the basin blue.

The doors lilac.

And that is all - there is nothing in this room with closed shutters.

The broad lines of the furniture must again express inviolable rest. Portraits on the walls, and a mirror and a towel and some clothes.

The frame - as there is no white in the picture - will be white.

This is by way of revenge for the enforced rest I have been obliged to take.

I shall work at it again all day tomorrow, but you see how simple the conception is. The shadows and the thrown shadows are suppressed, it is coloured in free flat tones like Japanese prints.   It is going to be a contrast with, for instance, the Tarascon diligence and the night café.

I am not writing you a long letter, because tomorrow very early I am going to begin in the cool morning light, so as to finish my canvas.

How are the pains? Do not forget to tell me about them.

I hope that you will write one of these days.

I will make you sketches of the other rooms too some day.

With a good handshake,

Yours,

Vincent

THE AGE OF INNOCENCE

That evening he unpacked his books from London. The box was full of things he had been waiting for impatiently; a new volume of Herbert Spencer, another collection of the prolific Alphonse Daudet's brilliant tales, and a novel called *Middlemarch*, as to which there had lately been interesting things said in the reviews. He had declined three dinner invitations in favour of this feast; but though he turned the pages with the sensuous joy of the book-lover, he did not know what he was reading, and one book after another dropped from his hand. Suddenly, among them, he lit on a small volume of verse which he had ordered because the name had attracted him: *The House of Life*. He took it up, and found himself plunged in an atmosphere unlike any he had ever breathed in books; so warm, so rich, and yet so ineffably tender, that it gave a new and haunting beauty to the most elementary of human passions. All through the night he pursued through those enchanted pages the vision of a woman who had the face of Ellen Olenska; but when he woke the next morning, and looked out at the brownstone houses across the street, and thought of his desk in Mr Letterblair's office, and the family pew in Grace Church, his hour in the park of Skuytercliff became as far outside the pale of probability as the visions of the night.

'Mercy, how pale you look, Newland!' Janey commented over the coffee-cups at breakfast; and his mother added: 'Newland dear, I've noticed lately that you've been coughing; I do hope you're not letting yourself be overworked?' For it was the conviction of both ladies that, under the iron despotism of his senior partners, the young man's life was spent in the most exhausting professional labours - and he had never thought it necessary to undeceive them.

Edith Wharton

SPRING FEVER

There is probably something about men crossed in love which tends to draw them together, some subtle aura or emanation which tells them that they have found a kindred soul. At any rate, every time Lord Shortlands looked at Stanwood, he felt that, while Stanwood unquestionably resembled a hippopotamus in appearance, it would be a genuine pleasure to fraternize with him. And every time Stanwood looked at Lord Shortlands, it was to say to himself: 'Granted that this bimbo looks like a butler out on the loose, nevertheless something whispers to me that we could be friends.' But for a while they remained mute and aloof. It was only when London's first wasp thrust itself into the picture that the barriers fell.

One is inclined to describe this wasp as the Wasp of Fate. Only by supposing it an instrument of destiny can one account for its presence that morning in the small bar of Barribault's Hotel. Even in the country its arrival on the twelfth of May would have been unusual, the official wasping season not beginning till well on in July, and how it came to be in the heart of London's steel and brick at such a time is a problem from which speculation recoils.

Still there it was, and for a space it volplaned and looped the loop about Lord Shortlands's nose, occasioning him no little concern. It then settled down for a brief breather on the back of Stanwood's coat, and Lord Shortlands, feeling that this was an opportunity which might not occur again, remembered his swashing blow, like Gregory in *Romeo and Juliet*, and downed it in its tracks with a large, flat hand.

A buffet between the shoulder blades does something to a man who is drinking a cocktail at the moment. Stanwood choked and turned purple. Recovering his breath, he said (with some justice): 'Hey!' and Lord Shortlands hastened to explain. He said:

'Wasp.'

P.G. Wodehouse

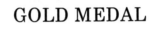

GOLD MEDAL

DOVER BEACH

The sea is calm to-night.
The tide is full, the moon lies fair
Upon the straits; - on the French coast the light
Gleams and is gone; the cliffs of England stand,
Glimmering and vast, out in the tranquil bay.
Come to the window, sweet is the night-air!
Only, from the long line of spray
Where the sea meets the moon-blanched land,
Listen! you hear the grating roar
Of pebbles which the waves draw back, and fling,
At their return, up the high strand,
Begin, and cease, and then again begin,
With tremulous cadence slow, and bring
The eternal note of sadness in.

Sophocles long ago
Heard it on the Ægæn, and it brought
Into his mind the turbid ebb and flow
Of human misery; we
Find also in the sound a thought,
Hearing it by this distant northern sea.

The Sea of Faith
Was once, too, at the full, and round earth's shore
Lay like the folds of a bright girdle furled.
But now I only hear
Its melancholy, long, withdrawing roar,
Retreating, to the breath
Of the night-wind, down the vast edges drear
And naked shingles of the world.

Ah, love, let us be true
To one another! for the world, which seems
To lie before us like a land of dreams,
So various, so beautiful, so new,

Hath really neither joy, nor love, nor light,
Nor certitude, nor peace, nor help for pain;
And we are here as on a darkling plain
Swept with confused alarms of struggle and flight,
Where ignorant armies clash by night.

Matthew Arnold

A STUDENT DRAMA GROUP PERFORMS IN AN OLD PEOPLE'S HOME

Early evening sun leaned through the window
And warmed the carpet under their bare feet.
Powder hazed the room, and make-up sticks
Jumped nervily from clutch to clutch. Clothing
Smothered chairs, and strained plastic bags
Burst in impatience spilling properties out.

Young men aged their temples, and girls
Trenched their incipient wrinkles with thick paint.
Outside the room the corridor unrolled
Itself to life, as walking frames and sticks
Hauled slow feet to this evening's destination.
Lost, querying voices wavered and fell,

Fell into silence in the dressing-room
Where ironies oozed tangible as sweat;
The low light from the window gilded arms
Roundly lifting from flurries of lawn, to crush
Bright hair under grey acrylic wigs.
They moved in mirrors with a shocked grace.

The cast followed the same corridor down
To the same end, to the room where the audience
Waited. Full-fleshed and springing under
Their flabby mimicry, they strode in

And hurried straight to the front to be looked at,
Vital, and shadowed now under a new guilt.

And afterwards the matron said that they
All had enjoyed it, residents and staff.
'And now I have to help to bed the ones
Who can't walk back to their little flats.
Thank you again, we like these changes here.
Next week, you know, we have the acrobats.'

John Cassidy

I CANNOT LIVE WITH YOU

I cannot live with You -
It would be Life -
And Life is over there -
Behind the Shelf

The Sexton keeps the Key to -
Putting up
Our Life - His Porcelain -
Like a Cup -

Discarded of the Housewife -
Quaint - or Broke -
A newer Sevres pleases -
Old Ones crack -

I could not die - with You -
For One must wait
To shut the Other's Gaze down -
You - could not -

And I - Could I stand by
And see You - freeze -
Without my Right of Frost -
Death's privilege?

Nor could I rise - with You -
Because Your Face
Would put out Jesus'-
That New Grace

Glow plain - and foreign
On my homesick Eye -
Except that You than He
Shone closer by -

They'd judge Us - How -
For You - served Heaven - You know,
Or sought to -
I could not -

Because You saturated Sight -
And I had no more Eyes
For sordid excellence
As Paradise

And were You lost, I would be -
Though My Name
Rang loudest
On the Heavenly fame -

And were You - saved -
And I - condemned to be
Where You were not -
That self - were Hell to Me -

So We must meet apart -
You there - I - here -
With just the Door ajar
That Oceans are - and Prayer -
And that White Sustenance -
Despair -

Emily Dickinson

THE DEFINITION OF LOVE

My love is of a birth as rare
As 'tis for object strange and high:
It was begotten by Despair
Upon Impossibility.

Magnanimous Despair alone
Could show me so divine a thing,
Where feeble Hope could ne'er have flown
But vainly flapped its tinsel wing.

And yet I quickly might arrive
Where my extended soul is fixed,
But Fate does iron wedges drive,
And always crowds itself betwixt.

For Fate with jealous eye does see
Two perfect loves, nor lets them close:
Their union would her ruin be,
And her tyrannic power depose.

And therefore her decrees of steel
Us as the distant Poles have placed,
(Though Love's whole world on us doth wheel)
Not by themselves to be embraced,

Unless the giddy heaven fall,
And earth some new convulsion tear;
And, us to join, the world should all
Be cramped into a planisphere.

As lines (so loves) oblique may well
Themselves in every angle greet:
But ours so truly parallel,
Though infinite, can never meet.

Therefore the love which us doth bind,
But Fate so enviously debars,
Is the conjunction of the mind,
And opposition of the stars.

Andrew Marvell

AN AFRICAN ELEGY

We are the miracles that God made
To taste the bitter fruit of Time.
We are precious.
And one day our suffering
Will turn into the wonders of the earth.

There are things that burn me now
Which turn golden when I am happy.
Do you see the mystery of our pain?
That we bear poverty
And are able to sing and dream sweet things

And that we never curse the air when it is warm
Or the fruit when it tastes so good
Or the lights that bounce gently on the waters?
We bless things even in our pain.
We bless them in silence.

That is why our music is so sweet.
It makes the air remember.
There are secret miracles at work
That only Time will bring forth.
I too have heard the dead singing

And they tell me that
This life is good
They tell me to live it gently
With fire, and always with hope.
There is wonder here

And there is surprise
In everything the unseen moves.
The ocean is full of songs.
The sky is not an enemy.
Destiny is our friend.

Ben Okhri

CHOCOLATES

Once some people were visting Chekhov.
While they made remarks about his genius
the Master fidgeted. Finally
he said, 'Do you like chocolates?'

They were astonished, and silent.
He repeated the question,
whereupon one lady plucked up her courage
and murmured shyly, 'Yes.'

'Tell me,' he said, leaning forward,
light glinting from his spectacles,
'what kind? The light, sweet chocolate
or the dark, bitter kind?'

The conversation became general.
They spoke of cherry centres,
of almonds and Brazil nuts.
Losing their inhibitions
they interrupted one another.
For people may not know what they think
about politics in the Balkans,
or the vexed question of men and women,

but everyone has a definite opinion
about the flavour of shredded coconut.
Finally someone spoke of chocolates filled with liqueur,
and everyone, even the author of *Uncle Vanya,*
was at a loss for words.

As they were leaving he stood by the door
and took their hands.
In the coach returning to Petersburg
they agreed that it had been a most
unusual conversation.

Louis Simpson

HISTORY AND REALITY

'Sin is nothing but the refusal to recognise human misery.'

SIMONE WEIL

I

Escaped from Germany -
Cared for by English friends, with whom
Kindness counted still -

Rumours reached her -

Photographs made by the Gestapo -

Jews, her people -
So various, all one -

Each taken full-face -

The strong - the meek - the sad - the proud.

*

Hunger had stretched the parchment skin
Across the contours of the bone -
Forehead, cheek-bones, chin.

And in each face there was the same
Ultimate revelation
Of eyes that stared upon the real -

Some terrible final thing.

II

She locked herself inside her room,
Her mind filled with those images
From Germany, her homeland, where
Those deaths were the reality -

Real! - not some tragedy that actors
Performed before an audience -
Pity and terror purifying
The onlooker, enraptured by
Poetry secreted in the lines.
But where the players were the victims
Massacred from a tyrant's mouth.

*

She felt a kind of envy for
Those who stood naked in their truth:
Where to be of her people was
To be one of those millions killed.

III

She starved her body to pure thought
To be one with her people snatched
From ghettos by the SS, then
Hurled into cattle trucks of trains
Hurtling all night across bare plains
Till dawn, when there stood, waiting on
Platforms of sidings (below walls
Of concrete and barbed wire) - guards, who
Marched them to a parade-ground, where
Those fit to work in factories
Were separated from the rest -
Women and children, the old, the sick,
Who, taken to a yard, were robbed
Of jewellery, satchels, playthings, shoes -

Things that to them meant home and name -
And made to stand there when a voice
From a watch-tower proclaimed they would
Be cleansed of lice, and being Jews.

IV

Then thrust inside a shed where she
Through her intense imagining
Stood there among them bodily
When, from outside, the guards turned on
Taps through which hissed not water but
The murdering gas, whereon that crowd
Breathed a great sigh of revelation -
Their life, their death - for her the real
Instant where history ground its wheel
On her with them, inside that moment
When - outside - truth was only words.

Stephen Spender

EPHEMERA

'Your eyes that once were never weary of mine
Are bowed in sorrow under pendulous lids,
Because our love is waning.'
                              And then she:
'Although our love is waning, let us stand
By the lone border of the lake once more,
Together in that hour of gentleness
When the poor tired child, Passion, falls asleep.
How far away the stars seem, and how far
Is our first kiss, and ah, how old my heart!'

Pensive they paced along the faded leaves,
While slowly he whose hand held hers replied:
'Passion has often worn our wandering hearts.'

The woods were round them and the yellow leaves
Fell like faint meteors in the gloom, and once
A rabbit old and lame limped down the path;
Autumn was over him: and now they stood
On the lone border of the lake once more:
Turning, he saw that she had thrust dead leaves
Gathered in silence, dewy as her eyes,
In bosom and hair.

              'Ah, do not mourn,' he said,
'That we are tired, for other loves await us;
Hate on and love through unrepining hours.
Before us lies eternity; our souls
Are love, and a continual farewell.'

William Butler Yeats

CLAYHANGER

'Well?' Darius growled impatiently, even savagely. They saw each other, not once a week, but at nearly every hour of every day, and they were surfeited of the companionship.

'Supposing I wanted to get married?' This sentence shot out of Edwin's mouth like a bolt. And as it flew, he blushed very red. In the privacy of his mind he was horribly swearing.

'So that's it, is it?' Darius growled again. And he leaned forward and picked up the poker, not as a menace, but because he too was nervous. As an opposer of his son he had never had quite the same confidence in himself since Edwin's historic fury at being suspected of theft, though apparently their relations had resumed the old basis of bullying and submission.

'Well -' Edwin hesitated. He thought, 'after all, people do get married. It won't be a crime.'

'Who'st been running after?' Darius demanded inimically. Instead of being softened by this rumour of love, by this hint that his son had been passing through wondrous secret hours, he instinctively and without any reason hardened himself and transformed the news into an offence. He felt no sympathy and it did not occur to him to recall that he too had once thought of marrying. He was a man whom life had brutalized about half a century earlier.

'I was only thinking,' said Edwin clumsily - the fool had not sense enough even to sit down - 'I was only thinking, suppose I did want to get married.'

'Who'st been running after?'

'Well, I can't rightly say there's anything - what you may call settled. In fact, nothing was to be said about it all at present. But it's Miss Lessways, father - Hilda Lessways, you know.'

'Her as came in the shop the other day?'

'Yes.'

'How long's this been going on?'

Edwin thought of what Hilda had said. 'Oh! Over a year.'
He could not possibly have said 'four days'. 'Mind you this is
strictly q.t.! Nobody knows a word about it, nobody! But of course
I thought I'd better tell you. You'll say nothing.' He tried wist-
fully to appeal as one loyal man to another. But he failed. There
was no ray of response on his father's gloomy features, and he
slipped back insensibly into the boy whose right to an individual
existence had never been formally admitted.

Arnold Bennett

LOOK AT ME

There was no one in sight. There was no sound, apart from
a distant rumble, which I could not identify. I was breathing
harshly now and I could feel a pain in my chest; my hair stuck
to my damp face in wisps, and I was very thirsty. The dull
rumble came nearer, and I was aware of a dark shape looming
in front of me, high above. Then I realised that this was the
flyover, and that I should have to negotiate another underpass
in order to get to the other side, and home.

For some time I could not do it. I clung to the railings and
waited to feel better, and still did nothing. I think I even decided
that I might stay there until someone came along and then I
might summon up the courage to follow them down those steps.
I was prepared to wait until the morning, but I was so tired, and
it was so dark, that this immediately became unimaginable.
Several times I started down the steps, only to retreat to the
surface, my mouth dry. I could not go down there. I knew that
people sometimes slept rough in subways, that they were the
favourite haunt of drunks and derelicts. I thought of the man at
Marble Arch and I smelt the smell again. I think at one point
that I must have sat down on the steps and buried my face in my
hands. I had never had to do this before, on my own. James,
who knew I was frightened, had always put his arm round me,

and that way it was even enjoyable. And thus I felt his loss again, and the loss of all protection, and I tried to summon the compensating anger. But at some point on that homeward journey, even the anger had retreated from my grasp.

And then, after about half an hour, I managed to go down the steps. But I was shaking so much that I had to cling to the railing, feeling for every step with my foot, and then, when I had reached the tunnel, keeping close to the wall, the dirty tiles, ready at the slightest sound to retreat, or, when I had passed the halfway mark, to fling myself forward. It took a long time, that I know; I also know that when I reached the steps at the other end I could hardly lift my feet to climb them. At one point I was overcome with a sort of vertigo and had to stand still until I found the will to go on. I emerged upwards into the blackest night I had ever seen.

Anita Brookner

WHERE ANGELS FEAR TO TREAD

Lilia, so similar to her husband in many ways, yearned for comfort and sympathy too. The night he laughed at her she wildly took up paper and pen and wrote page after page, analysing his character, enumerating his iniquities, reporting whole conversations, tracing all the causes and the growth of her misery. She was beside herself with passion, and though she could hardly think or see, she suddenly attained to magnificence and pathos which a practised stylist might have envied. It was written like a diary, and not till its conclusion did she realize for whom it was meant.

'Irma, darling Irma, this letter is for you. I almost forget I have a daughter. It will make you unhappy, but I want you to know everything, and you cannot learn things too soon. God bless you, my dearest, and save you. God bless your miserable mother.'

Fortunately Mrs Herriton was in when the letter arrived. She seized it and opened it in her bedroom. Another moment, and Irma's placid childhood would have been destroyed for ever.

Lilia received a brief note from Harriet, again forbidding direct communication between mother and daughter, and concluding with formal condolences. It nearly drove her mad.

'Gently! gently!' said her husband. They were sitting together on the loggia when the letter arrived. He often sat with her now, watching her for hours, puzzled and anxious, but not contrite.

'It's nothing.' She went in and tore it up, and then began to write - a very short letter, whose gist was 'Come and save me.'

It is not good to see your wife crying when she writes - especially if you are conscious that, on the whole, your treatment of her has been reasonable and kind. It is not good, when you accidentally look over her shoulder, to see that she is writing to a man. Nor should she shake her fist at you when she leaves the room, under the impression that you are engaged in lighting a cigar and cannot see her.

E.M. Forster

THE LEOPARD

The Prince had always taken care that the first dinner at Donnafugata should bear the stamp of solemnity: children under fifteen were excluded from table, French wines were served, there was punch *alla Romana* before the roast; and the flunkeys were in powder and knee-breeches. On just one detail did he compromise; he never wore evening dress, lest he embarrass guests who would, obviously, possess none. That evening, in the "Leopold" drawing-room, as it was called, the Salina family were awaiting the last arrivals. From under lace-covered shades the oil-lamps spread circumscribed yellow light: the vast equestrian portraits of past Salinas were as imposing and shadowy as their memories. Don Onofrio had arrived with his wife, and so had the arch-priest who, with his light mantle folded back on his shoulders in sign of gala, was telling the Princess about tiffs at the College of Mary. Don Ciccio, the organist, had also arrived (Teresina had already been tied to the leg of a scullery table) and was recalling with the Prince their fantastic bags in the Dragonara ravines. All was placid and normal when Francesco Paolo, the sixteen-year-old son, burst into the room and announced: 'Papa, Don Calogero is just coming up the stairs. In *tails!*'

Tancredi, intent on fascinating the wife of Don Onofrio, realised the import of the news a second before the others. But when he heard that fatal word he could not contain himself and burst into convulsive laughter. No laugh, though, came from the Prince on whom, one might almost say, this news had more effect than the bulletin about Garibaldi's landing at Marsala. That had been an event not only foreseen but also distant and invisible. Now, with his sensibility to presages and symbols, he saw revolution in that white tie and two black tails moving at this moment up the stairs of his own home. Not only was he, the Prince, no longer the major landowner in Donnafugata, but he now found himself forced to receive, when in afternoon dress himself, a guest appearing in evening clothes.

Giuseppe Tomasi di Lampedusa

TITUS GROAN

As his lordship stared at the doctor another figure appeared, a girl of about fifteen with long, rather wild black hair. She was gauche in movement and in a sense, ugly of face, but with how small a twist might she not suddenly have become beautiful. Her sullen mouth was full and rich - her eyes smouldered.

A yellow scarf hung loosely around her neck. Her shapeless dress was a flaming red.

For all the straightness of her back she walked with a slouch.

'Come here,' said Lord Groan as she was about to pass him and the doctor.

'Yes father,' she said huskily.

'Where have you been for the last fortnight, Fuchsia?'

'Oh, here and there, father,' she said, staring at her shoes.

She tossed her long hair and it flapped down her back like a pirate's flag. She stood in about as awkward a manner as could be conceived. Utterly un-feminine - no man could have invented it.

'Here and there?' echoed her father in a weary voice. 'What does "here and there" mean? You've been in hiding. Where, girl?'

' 'N the libr'y and 'n the armoury, 'n walking about a lot', said Lady Fuchsia, and her sullen eyes narrowed. 'I just heard silly rumours about mother. They said I've got a brother - idiots! idiots! I hate them. I haven't, have I? Have I?'

'A little brother', broke in Doctor Prunesquallor. 'Yes, ha, ha, ha, ha, ha, ha, ha, a minute, infinitesimal, microscopic addition to the famous line is now behind this bedroom door. Ha, ha, ha, ha, ha, ha, he, he, he! Oh yes! Ha, ha! Oh yes indeed! Very much so.'

'No!' said Fuchsia so loudly that the doctor coughed crisply and his lordship took a step forward with his eyebrows drawn together and a sad curl at the corner of his mouth.

'It's not true!' shouted Fuchsia, turning from them and twirling a great lock of black hair round and round her wrist. 'I don't believe it! Let me go! Let me go!'

As no one was touching her, her cry was unnecessary and she turned and ran with strange bounds along the corridor that led from the landing. Before she was lost to view, Steerpike could hear her voice shouting from the distance, 'Oh how I hate! hate! hate! How I *hate* people! Oh how I *hate* people!'

Mervyn Peake

THE PIGEON

The clochard on the bench across the way had finished his meal. After the sardines and the bread, he had dined on cheese, pears, and biscuits as well, taken a big pull on his wine bottle, given a sigh of deep contentment, and rolled his jacket into a pillow, bedding his head on it, stretching his lazy, satiated body out on the bench for a midday nap. Now he slept. Sparrows came over to peck away at the breadcrumbs, then, attracted by the sparrows, pigeons waddled their way to the bench to hack with their black beaks at the sardine heads that had been bitten off. The clochard did not let the birds disturb him. He slept soundly and peacefully.

Jonathan watched him. And as he watched him, a strange disquiet came over him. the disquiet was nor fed by envy as in the old days, but by amazement: how was it possible - he asked himself - that this man, well over fifty now, was still alive at all? Given his thoroughly irresponsible way of life, should he not long ago have starved or frozen to death, been cut down by cirrhosis of the liver - be dead at any rate? Instead, he ate and drank with the best of appetites, slept the sleep of the just and, wearing a cotton jacket and patched trousers - which of course had long ago replaced those that he had pulled down on the rue Daupin, relatively smart, almost fashionable corduroy trousers, apart from a repair here and there - gave the impression of a firmly grounded personality in finest harmony with the world and enjoying life... whereas he, Jonathan - and his amazement gradually mounted to a kind of nervous bewilderment - whereas he, who his whole life long had been a well-behaved and orderly fellow, unpretentious, almost ascetic, clean, always punctual and obedient, reliable, respectable... and every sou he had earned himself, and always paid cash, for his utility bill, his rent, the concierge's Christmas tip... and never incurred debts, never been a burden to anyone, never once been sick or cost social service agencies a centime,,, never done anything to huirt anyone, had never, ever wanted anything from life except to maintain and guarantee his own modest, small contentment of soul... whereas he now saw himself, at the age of fifty three, plunging head over heels into a crisis that confounded the life's plan he had devised for himself and was making him crazy and confused and had him eating raisin rolls for the pure confusion of it, and for fright. Yes, he was frightened!

Patrick Süskind

Translated by John E. Woods

THE SECRET HISTORY

A sudden wind rustled through the birches; a gust of yellow leaves came storming down. I took a sip of my drink. If I had grown up in that house I couldn't have loved it more, couldn't have been more familiar with the creak of the swing, or the pattern of the clematis vines on the trellis, or the velvety swell of land as it faded to gray on the horizon, and the strip of highway visible - just barely - in the hills, beyond the trees. The very colors of the place had seeped into my blood: just as Hampden, in subsequent years, would always present itself immediately to my imagination in a confused whirl of white and green and red, so the country house first appeared as a glorious blur of water-colors, of ivory and lapis blue, chestnut and burnt orange and gold, separating only gradually into the boundaries of remembered objects: the house, the sky, the maple trees. But even that day, there on the porch, with Charles beside me and the smell of wood smoke in the air, it had the quality of a memory; there it was, before my eyes, and yet too beautiful to believe.

It was getting dark; soon it would be time for dinner. I finished my drink in a swallow. The idea of living there, of not having to go back ever again to asphalt and shopping malls and modular furniture; of living there with Charles and Camilla and

Henry and Francis and maybe even Bunny; of no one marrying or going home or getting a job in a town a thousand miles away or doing any of the traitorous things friends do after college; of everything remaining exactly as it was, that instant - the idea was so truly heavenly that I'm not sure I thought, even then, it could ever really happen, but I like to believe I did.

Francis was working up to a big finish on his song. " 'Gentlemen songsters *off* on a spree... Doomed from here to *eter*nity...' "

Charles looked at me sideways. "So, what about you?" he said.

"What do you mean?"

"I mean, do you have any plans?" He laughed. "What are you doing for the next forty or fifty years of your life?"

Out on the lawn, Bunny had just knocked Henry's ball about seventy feet outside the court. There was a ragged burst of laughter; faint, but clear, it floated back across the evening air. That laughter haunts me still.

Donna Tartt

DECLINE AND FALL

That evening Paul received a summons from the Doctor. He wore a double-breasted dinner-jacket, which he smoothed uneasily over his hips at Paul's approach. He looked worried and old.

'Pennyfeather,' he said, 'I have this morning received a severe shock, two shocks in fact. The first was disagreeable, but not wholly unexpected. Your colleague, Captain Grimes, has been convicted before me, on evidence that leaves no possibility of his innocence, of a crime - I might almost call it a course of action - which I can neither understand nor excuse. I dare say I need not particularize. I discerned Captain Grimes' weakness early in our acquaintance and a man of your intelligence and sensibility living at close quarters with him can scarcely have done otherwise also. But I had hoped, I had fondly hoped, that I might be spared the unpleasantness of a public denunciation. However, that is all a minor question. I have quite frequently met with similar cases during a long experience in our profession. But what has disturbed and grieved me more than I can moderately express is the information that he is engaged to be married to my elder daughter. That, Pennyfeather, I had not expected. In the circumstances, it seemed a humiliation I might reasonably have been spared. I tell you all this, Pennyfeather, because in our brief acquaintance I have learned to trust and respect you.'

The Doctor sighed, drew from his pocket a handkerchief of *crêpe de chine*, blew his nose with every accent of emotion, and resumed:

'He is *not* the son-in-law I should readily have chosen. I could have forgiven him his wooden leg, his slavish poverty, his moral turpitude, and his abominable features; I could even have forgiven him his incredible vocabulary, if only he had been a *gentleman*. I hope you do not think me a snob. You may have discerned in me a certain prejudice against the lower orders. It is quite true. I *do* feel deeply on the subject. You see, I married one of them.'

Evelyn Waugh

LICENTIATE TEACHERS' DIPLOMA

THE WANDERER

Doom is dark and deeper than any sea-dingle.
Upon what man it fall
In spring, day-wishing flowers appearing,
Avalanche sliding, white snow from rock-face,
That he should leave his house,
No cloud-soft hand can hold him, restraint by women;
But ever that man goes
Through place-keepers, through forest trees,
A stranger to strangers over undried sea,
Houses for fishes, suffocating water,
Or lonely on fell as chat,
By pot-holed becks
A bird stone-haunting, an unquiet bird.

There head falls forward, fatigued at evening,
And dreams of home,
Waving from window, spread of welcome,
Kissing of wife under single sheet;
But waking sees
Bird-flocks nameless to him, through doorway voices
Of new men making another love.

Save him from hostile capture,
From sudden tiger's leap at corner;
Protect his house,
His anxious house where days are counted
From thunderbolt protect,
From gradual ruin spreading like a stain;
Converting number from vague to certain,
Bring joy, bring day of his returning,
Lucky with day approaching, with leaning dawn.

W.H. Auden

JUST STANDING THERE

It's a wooden bridge, an ordinary bridge,
A small one, on which I've stood many times,
Looking into the fast, earthy water, watching
Oddments sail by, rose-prunings from an upstream garden,
Twigs, litter, sometimes a flowerhead, observing
Waterside botany immersed, dragged, but never drowned.
For years, though, I crossed the stream on my daily walk,
Ignoring that deep burn, or glancing at it.
Then I took to leaning on the timber parapet,
Staring into the fishless flood - or I've seen no fish
Ever in hundreds of quiet lookings, and if it dwindles
In summer, it is not by much, just enough
For an inch or two of bank to dry out, for a tuft
To lift its hair up from the tugging, onward rinse.
Insignificant, small, an ordinary wooden bridge,
It became a platform for a fifteen-minute staring
Into liquid muscle, a stamina that no one has
In mind or body - cliché of even little rivers
Or any patch of ground, stone, or man-outliving tree.
Commonplace as it is, it still took years to learn;
It took years to hear its several pitches of babble,
Watery lore encompassing tenderness and rage,
Always the same water, and never the same.
This is not an ordinary, small, wooden bridge.
It doesn't cross from reality to spirit,
But, in the middle, where I stand, leaning on the parapet,
Silent truth in me listens to a running giant
Let loose in unclocked liberty, as free as water
Drugged with its destination in the firth and sea.
It's not my burn. Nothing like this is mine, it tells me.
And as for the bridge, it belongs to the municipality.
Reality is yours, and your spirit is your own.
Stand here, or anywhere, long enough, and you will learn that.
It's not the stream or the bridge; it's where I stand

At a precise spot of nowhere and timelessness
Within myself, a door I can go through and be invisible
In a room also invisible or from which I come back
Without memory other than languageless noise in the ears
Such as can be recalled clearly but never spoken.

Douglas Dunn

WODWO

What am I? Nosing here, turning leaves over
Following a faint stain on the air to the river's edge
I enter water. What am I to split
The glassy grain of water looking upward I see the bed
Of the river above me upside down very clear
What am I doing here in mid-air? Why do I find
this frog so interesting as I inspect its most secret
interior and make it my own? Do these weeds
know me and name me to each other have they
seen me before, do I fit in their world? I seem
separate from the ground and not rooted but dropped
out of nothing casually I've no threads
fastening me to anything I can go anywhere
I seem to have been given the freedom
of this place what am I then? And picking
bits of bark off this rotten stump gives me
no pleasure and it's no use so why do I do it
me and doing that have coincided very queerly
But what shall I be called am I the first
have I an owner what shape am I what
shape am I am I huge if I go
to the end on this way past these trees and past these trees
till I get tired that's touching one wall of me
for the moment if I sit still how everything
stops to watch me I suppose I am the exact centre

but there's all this what is it roots
roots roots roots and here's the water
again very queer but I'll go on looking

Ted Hughes

DOCKERY AND SON

'Dockery was junior to you,
Wasn't he?' said the Dean. 'His son's here now.'
Death-suited, visitant, I nod. 'And do
You keep in touch with - ' Or remember how
Black-gowned, unbreakfasted,and still half-tight
We used to stand before that desk, to give
'Our version' of 'these incidents last night'?
I try the door of where I used to live:

Locked. The lawn spreads dazzlingly wide.
A known bell chimes. I catch my train, ignored.
Canal and clouds and colleges subside
Slowly from view. But Dockery, good Lord,
Anyone up today must have been born
In '43, when I was twenty-one.
If he was younger, did he get this son
At nineteen, twenty? Was he that withdrawn

High-collared public-schoolboy, sharing rooms
With Cartwright who was killed? Well, it just shows
How much . . . How little . . . Yawning, I suppose
I fell asleep, waking at the fumes
And furnace-glares of Sheffield, where I changed,
And ate an awful pie, and walked along
The platform to its end to see the ranged
Joining and parting lines reflect a strong

Unhindered moon. To have no son, no wife,
No house or land still seemed quite natural.
Only a numbness registered the shock
Of finding out how much had gone of life,
How widely from the others. Dockery, now:
Only nineteen, he must have taken stock
Of what he wanted, and been capable
Of . . . No, that's not the difference: rather, how

Convinced he was he should be added to!
Why did he think adding meant increase?
To me it was dilution. Where do these
Innate assumptions come from? Not from what
We think truest, or most want to do:
Those warp tight-shut, like doors. They're more a style
Our lives bring with them: habit for a while,
Suddenly they harden into all we've got

And how we got it; looked back on, they rear
Like sand-clouds, thick and close, embodying
For Dockery a son, for me nothing,
Nothing with all a son's harsh patronage.
Life is first boredom, then fear.
Whether or not we use it, it goes,
Ad leaves what something hidden from us chose,
And age, and then the only end of age.

Philip Larkin

BAVARIAN GENTIANS

Not every man has gentians in his house
in Soft September, at slow, Sad Michaelmas.

Bavarian gentians, big and dark, only dark
darkening the day-time torch-like with the smoking blueness
    of Pluto's gloom,
ribbed and torch-like, with their blaze of darkness spread blue
down flattening into points, flattened under the sweep of
    white day
torch-flower of the blue-smoking darkness, Pluto's dark-blue
    daze,
black lamps from the halls of Dio, burning dark blue,
giving off darkness, blue darkness, as Demeter's pale lamps
    give off light,
lead me then, lead me the way.

Reach me a gentian, give me a torch
let me guide myself with the blue, forked torch of this flower
down the darker and darker stairs, where blue is darkened on
    blueness.
even where Persephone goes, just now, from the frosted
    September
to the sightless realm where darkness is awake upon the dark
and Persephone herself is but a voice
or a darkness invisible enfolded in the deeper dark
of the arms Plutonic, and pierced with the passion of dense
    gloom,
among the splendour of torches of darkness, shedding
    darkness on the lost bride and her groom.

D.H. Lawrence

from HERO AND LEANDER

By this, sad Hero, with love unacquainted,
Viewing Leander's face, fell down and fainted.
He kiss'd her, and breath'd life into her lips;
Wherewith, as one displeas'd, away she trips;
Yet, as she went, full often look'd behind,
And many poor excuses did she find
To linger by the way, and once she stay'd,
And would have turn'd again, but was afraid,
In offering parley, to be counted light:
So on she goes, and, in her idle flight,
Her painted fan of curled plumes let fall,
Thinking to train Leander therewithal.
He, being a novice, knew not what she meant,
But stay'd, and after her a letter sent;
Which joyful Hero answer'd in such sort,
As he had hope to scale the beauteous fort
Wherein the liberal Graces lock'd their wealth;
And therefore to her tower he got by stealth.
Wide-open stood the door; he need not climb;
And she herself, before the pointed time,
Had spread the board, with roses strew'd the room,
And oft look'd out, and mus'd he did not come.
At last he came: O, who can tell the greeting
These greedy lovers had at their first meeting?
He ask'd; she gave; and nothing was denied;
Both to each other quickly were affied:
Look how their hands, so were their hearts united,
And what he did she willingly requited.
(Sweet are the kisses, the embracements sweet,
When like desires and affections meet;
For from the earth to heaven is Cupid rais'd,
Where fancy is in equal balance pais'd.)
Yet she this rashness suddenly repented,
And turn'd aside, and to herself lamented,

As if her name and honour had been wrong'd,
By being possess'd of him for whom she long'd;
Ay, and she wish'd, albeit not from her heart,
That he would leave her turret and depart.
The mirthful god of amorous pleasure smil'd
To see how he this captive nymph beguil'd;
For hitherto he did but fan the fire,
And kept it down, that it might mount the higher.
Now wax'd she jealous lest his love abated,
Fearing her own thoughts made her to be hated.
Thereforeunto him hastily she goes,
And, like light Salmacis, her body throws
Upon his bosom, where with yielding eyes
She offers up herself a sacrifice.

Christopher Marlowe

A HOUSE OF MERCY

It was a house of female habitation,
Two ladies fair inhabited the house,
And they were brave. For although Fear knocked loud
Upon the door, and said he must come in,
They did not let him in.

There were also two feeble babes, two girls,
That Mrs S. had by her husband had,
He soon left them and went away to sea,
Nor sent them money, nor came home again
Except to borrow back
Her Naval Officer's Wife's Allowance from Mrs S.
Who gave it him at once, she thought she should.

There was also the ladies' aunt
And babes' great aunt, a Mrs Martha Hearn Clode,
And she was elderly.
These ladies put their money all together
And so we lived.

I was the younger of the feeble babes
And when I was a child my mother died
And later Great Aunt Martha Hearn Clode died
And later still my sister went away.

Now I am old I tend my mother's sister
The noble aunt who so long tended us,
Faithful and True her name is. Tranquil
Also Sardonic. And I tend the house.

It is a house of female habitation
A house expecting strength as it is strong
A house of aristocratic mould that looks apart
When tears fall; counts despair
Derisory. Yet it has kept us well. For all its faults,
If they are faults, of sternness and reserve,
It is a Being of warmth I think; at heart
A house of mercy.

Stevie Smith

A SEA-CHANTEY

Là, tout n'est qu'ordre et beauté,
Luxe, calme, et volupté.

Anguilla, Adina,
Antigua, Cannelles,
Andreuille, all the l's,
Voyelles, of the liquid Antilles,
The names tremble like needles
Of anchored frigates,
Yachts tranquil as lilies,
In ports of calm coral,
The lithe, ebony hulls
Of strait-stitching schooners,
The needles of their masts
That thread archipelagoes
Refracted embroidery
In feverish waters
Of the sea-farer's islands,
Their shorn, leaning palms,
Shaft of Odysseus,
Cyclopic volcanoes,
Creak their own histories,
In the peace of green anchorage;
Flight, and Phyllis,
Returned from the Grenadines,
Names entered this sabbath,
In the port-clerk's register;
Their baptismal names,
The sea's liquid letters,
Repos donnez a cils ...
And their blazing cargoes
Of charcoal and oranges;
Quiet, the fury of their ropes.

Daybreak is breaking
On the green chrome water,
The white herons of yachts
Are at sabbath communion,
The histories of schooners
Are murmured in coral,
Their cargoes of sponges
On sandspits of islets
Barques white as white salt
Of acrid Saint Maarten,
Hulls crusted with barnacles,
Holds foul with great turtles,
Whose ship-boys have seen
The blue heave of Leviathan,
A sea-faring, Christian,
And intrepid people.
Now an apprentice washes his cheeks
With salt water and sunlight.

In the middle of the harbour
A fish breaks the Sabbath
With a silvery leap.
The scales fall from him
In a tinkle of church-bells;
The town streets are orange
With the week-ripened sunlight,
Balanced on the bowsprit
A young sailor is playing
His grandfather's chantey
On a trembling mouth-organ.
The music curls, dwindling
Like smoke from blue galleys,
To dissolve near the mountains.
The music uncurls with
The soft vowels of inlets,

The christening of vessels,
The titles of portages,
The colours of sea-grapes,
The tartness of sea-almonds,
The alphabet of church-bells,
The peace of white horses,
The pastures of ports,
The litany of islands,
Therosary of archipelagoes,
Anguilla, Antigua,
Virgin of Guadeloupe,
And stone-white Grenada
Of sunlight and pigeons,
The amen of calm waters,
The amen of calm waters,
The amen of calm waters.

Derek Walcott

LONDON FIELDS

TV AND DARTS, said the sign. AND PIMBALL. The first time Guy entered the Black Cross he was a man pushing through the black door of his fear ... He survived. He lived. The place was ruined and innocuous in its northern light: a clutch of dudes and Rastas playing pool over the damp swipe of the baize, the pewtery sickliness of the whites (they looked like war footage), the twittering fruit-machines, the fuming pie-warmer. Guy asked for a drink in the only voice he had: he didn't tousle his hair or his accent; he carried no tabloid under his arm, open on the racing page. With a glass of medium-sweet white wine he moved to the pinball table, an old Gottlieb, with Arabian Nights artwork (temptress, devil, hero, maiden) - Eye of the Tiger. Eye of the Tiger... A decrepit Irish youth stood inches away whispering *who's the boss who's the boss* into Guy's ear for as long as he seemed to need to do that. Whenever Guy looked up a dreadful veteran of the pub, his face twanging in the canned rock, stared at him bitterly, like the old man you stop for at the zebra who crosses slowly, with undiminished suspicion: no forgiveness there, not ever. The incomprehensible accusations of a sweat-soaked black girl were finally silenced by a five-pound note. Guy stayed for half an hour, and got out. He took so much fear away with him that there had to be less of it each time he returned. But going there at night was another entry.

Keith was the key: Keith, and his pub charisma. Keith was the pub champ. The loudest, the most booming in his shouts for more drink, the most violent in his abuse of the fruit machine, the best at darts - a darts force in the Black Cross... Now plainly Keith had to do something about Guy, who was far too anomalous to be let alone, with his pub anticharisma. Keith had to ban him, befriend him, beat him up. Kill him. So he pouched his darts one day and walked the length of the bar (regulars were wondering when it would happen), leaned over the pinball table with an

eyebrow raised and his tongue between his teeth: and bought
Guy a drink. The hip pocket, the furled tenners. Keith's house
had many mansions. The whole pub shook with silent applause.

Martin Amis

THE LIFE OF SAMUEL JOHNSON

We went home to his house for tea. Mrs Williams made it
with sufficient dexterity, notwithstanding her blindness, though
her manner of satisfying herself that the cups were full enough
appeared to me a little awkward; for I fancied she put her finger
down a certain way, till she felt the tea touch it. In my first
elation at being allowed the privilege of attending Dr Johnson at
his late visits to this lady, which was like being *è secretoribus
consiliis*, I willingly drank cup after cup, as if it had been of the
Heliconian spring. But as the charm of novelty went off, I grew
more fastidious; and besides, I discovered that she was of a
peevish temper.

There was a pretty large circle this evening. Dr Johnson was
in a very good humour, lively, and ready to talk upon all subjects.
Mr Fergusson, the self-taught philosopher, told him of a new
invented machine which went without horses; a man who sat in
it turned a handle, which worked a spring that drove it forward.
'Then, Sir,' said Johnson, 'what is gained is, the man has his
choice whether he will move himself alone, or himself and the
machine too.' Domenicetti being mentioned, he would not allow
him any merit. 'There is nothing in all this boasted system. No,
Sir, medicated baths can be no better than warm water; their
only effect can be that of tepid moisture.' One of the company
took the other side, maintaining that medicines of various sorts,
and some too of the most powerful effect, are introduced into the
human frame by the medium of the pores; and, therefore, when
warm water is impregnated with salutiferous substances, it may

produce great effects as a bath. This appeared to me very satisfactory. Johnson did not answer it; but talking for victory, and determined to be master of the field, he had recourse to the device which Goldsmith imputed to him in the witty words of one of Cibber's comedies: 'There is no arguing with Johnson; for when his pistol misses fire, he knocks you down with the butt-end of it.' He turned to the gentleman, 'Well, Sir, go to Dominicetti, and get thyself fumigated; but be sure that the steam be directed to thy *head*, for *that* is the *peccant part.*' This produced a triumphant roar of laughter from the motley assembly of philosophers, printers and dependents, male and female.

James Boswell

WILD SWANS

'How dare you challenge Chairman Mao's words!' exclaimed Mrs Ting. 'Deputy Commander Lin Biao said: "Every word of Chairman Mao's is universal absolute truth, and every word equals ten thousand words"!'

'If a word means one word,' my father said, 'it is already a man's supreme achievement. It is not humanly possible for one word to mean ten thousand. What Deputy Commander Lin Biao said was rhetorical, and should not be taken literally.'

The Tings could not believe their ears, according to their account afterward. They warned my father that his way of thinking, talking, and behaving was against the Cultural Revolution, which was led by Chairman Mao. To this my father said he would like a chance to debate with Chairman Mao about the whole thing. These words were so suicidal that the Tings were speechless. After a silence, they stood up to leave.

My grandmother heard angry footsteps and rushed out of the kitchen, her hands dusted with wheat flour into which she had been dipping the dumplings. She collided with Mrs Ting and asked the couple to stay for lunch. Mrs Ting ignored her, stormed out of the apartment, and started to tramp downstairs. At the landing she stopped, turned around, and said furiously to my father, who had come out with them, 'Are you crazy? I'm asking you for the last time: Do you still refuse my help? You realize I can do anything to you now.'

'I want nothing to do with you,' my father said. 'You and I are different species.'

Leaving my startled and fearful grandmother at the top of the stairs, my father went into his study. He came out almost at once, and carried an inkstone to the bathroom. He dripped a few drops of water onto the stone and walked thoughtfully back into the study. Then he sat down at his desk, and started grinding a stick of ink round and round the stone, forming a thick black liquid. He spread a blank sheet of paper in front of him. In no time, he had finished his second letter to Mao. He started by saying: 'Chairman Mao, I appeal to you, as one Communist to another, to stop the Cultural Revolution.' He went on to describe the disasters into which it had thrown China. The letter ended with the words: 'I fear the worst for our Party and our country if people like Liu Jie-ting and Zhang Xi-ting are given power over the lives of tens of millions of people.

He addressed the envelope to 'Chairman Mao, Peking,' and took it to the post office at the top of the street. He sent it by registered airmail. The clerk behind the counter took the envelope and glanced at it, maintaining an expression of total blankness. Then my father walked home - to wait.

Jung Chang

BLEAK HOUSE

"You wouldn't allow me to offer you one, would you, miss?" said Mr. Guppy, apparently refreshed.

"Not any," said I.

"Not half a glass?" said Mr. Guppy; "quarter? No! Then to proceed. My present salary, Miss Summerson, at Kenge and Carboy's, is two pound a week. When I first had the happiness of looking upon you, it was one-fifteen, and had stood at that figure for a lengthened period. A rise of five has since taken place, and a further rise of five is guaranteed at the expiration of a term not exceeding twelve months from the present date. My mother has a little property, which takes the form of a small life annuity; upon which she lives in an independent though unassuming manner, in the Old Street Road. She is eminently calculated for a mother-in-law. She never interferes, is all for peace, and her disposition easy. She has her failings - and who has not? - but I never knew her do it when company was present; at which time you may freely trust her with wines, spirits, or malt liquors. My own abode is lodgings at Penton Place, Pentonville. It is lowly, but airy, open at the back, and considered one of the 'ealthiest outlets. Miss Summerson! In the mildest language, I adore you. Would you be so kind as to allow me (as I may say) to file a declaration - to make an offer!"

Mr. Guppy went down on his knees. I was well behind my table, and not much frightened. I said, "Get up from that ridiculous position immediately, sir, or you will oblige me to break my implied promise and ring the bell!"

"Hear me out, miss!" said Mr. Guppy, folding his hands.

"I cannot consent to hear another word, sir," I returned, unless you get up from the carpet directly, and go and sit down at the table, as you ought to do if you have any sense at all."

He looked piteously, but slowly rose and did so.

"Yet what a mockery it is, miss," he said, with his hand upon his heart, and shaking his head at me in a melancholy manner over the tray, "to be stationed behind food at such a moment. The soul recoils from food at such a moment, miss."

Charles Dickens

FOUCAULT'S PENDULUM

In the center of the choir, in the flickering of the lanterns, something stirred, a slender shadow.

The Pendulum! The Pendulum no longer swayed in its familiar place in the center of the transept. A larger version of it had been hung from the keystone in the center of the choir. The sphere was larger; the wire much thicker, like a hawser, I thought, or a cable of braided metal strands. The Pendulum, now enormous, must have appeared in this way in the Panthéon. It was like beholding the moon through a telescope.

They had re-created the pendulum that the Templars first experimented with, half a millennium before Foucault. To allow it to sway freely, they had removed some ribs and supporting beams, turning the amphitheater of the choir into a crude symmetrical antistrophe marked out by the lanterns.

I asked myself how the Pendulum could maintain its constant oscillation, since the magnetic regulator could not be beneath it now, in the floor. Then I understood. At the edge of the choir, near the diesel engines, stood an individual ready to dart like a cat to follow the plane of oscillation. He gave the sphere a little push each time it came toward him, a precise light tap of the hand or the fingertips.

He was in tails, like Mandrake. Later, seeing his companions, I realized that he was indeed a magician, a prestidigitator from Le Petit Cirque of Madame Olcott; he was a professional, able to gauge pressures and distances, possessing a steady wrist skilled in working within the infinitesimal margins necessary in legerdemain. Perhaps through the thin soles of his gleaming shoes he could sense the vibrations of the currents, and move his hands according to the logic of both the sphere and the earth that governed it.

His companions - now I could see them as well. They moved among the automobiles in the nave, they scurried past the draisiennes and the motorcycles, almost tumbling in the shadows. Some carried a stool and a table covered with red cloth in the vast ambulatory in the rear, and some placed other lanterns. Tiny, nocturnal, twittering, they were like rachitic children, and as one went past me I saw mongoloid features and a bald head. Madame Olcott's Freaks Mignons, the horrible little monsters I had seen on the poster in the Librairie Sloane.

The circus was there in full force: the staff, guards, choreographers of the rite. I saw Alex and Denys, les Génts d'Avalon, sheathed in armor of studded leather. They were giants indeed, blond, leaning against the great bulk of the Obeissante, their arms folded as they waited.

I didn't have time to ask myself more questions. Someone had entered with solemnity, a hand extended to impose silence.

Umberto Eco

A GRIEF OBSERVED

Grief is like a long valley, a winding valley where any bend may reveal a totally new landscape. As I've already noted, not every bend does. Sometimes the surprise is the opposite one; you are presented with exactly the same sort of country you thought you had left behind miles ago. That is when you wonder whether the valley isn't a circular trench. But it isn't. There are partial recurrences, but the sequence doesn't repeat.

Here, for instance, is a new phase, a new loss. I do all the walking I can, for I'd be a fool to go to bed not tired. Today I have been revisiting old haunts, taking one of the long rambles that made me so happy in my bachelor days. And this time the face of nature was not emptied of its beauty and the world didn't look (as I complained some days ago) like a mean street. On the contrary, every horizon, every stile or clump of trees, summoned me into a past kind of happiness, my pre-H happiness. But the invitation seemed to me horrible. The happiness into which it invited me was insipid. I find that I don't want to go back again and be happy in that way. It frightens me to think that a mere going back should even be possible. For this fate would seem to me the worst of all; to reach a state in which my years of love and marriage should appear in retrospect a charming episode - like a holiday - that had briefly interrupted my interminable life and returned me to normal, unchanged. And then it would come to seem unreal - something so foreign to the usual texture of my history that I could almost believe it had happened to someone else. Thus H would die to me a second time; a worse bereavement than the first. Anything but that.

Did you ever know, dear, how much you took away with you when you left? You have stripped me even of my past, even of the things we never shared. I was wrong to say the stump was recovering from the pain of the amputation. I was deceived because it has so many ways to hurt me that I discover them only one by one.

C.S. Lewis

THE TOWERS OF SILENCE

She sat on the edge of the bed. She could not remember, now, ever being young. And then did. 'I was always a bit afraid of going upstairs to bed. So I hummed a song which I fear Mother disapproved. That is to say the first line of it. I don't mean she disapproved only of the first line and of course I don't mean hummed because you can't hum words, but I sang it under my breath over and over. And in the end I couldn't ever remember the rest of it and never have. Isn't that strange? I've seen a deal of gaiety throughout my noisy life.'

'Throughout what?'

'Throughout my noisy life.'

'Oh.' Mabel smiled. 'One of your father's comic songs.'

'He was passionately fond of the music hall. And often promised to take me but of course never did, he was afraid of what my mother would say if she found out and anyway he was always short of what he called the ready. There was the Christmas when he lost the presents for my stocking on the journey home. As white as a sheet when he came in at the door and very very late, but not drunk, that's what Mother said years later when she told me, when he was dead and she had forgiven him, and told me there wasn't any Father Christmas anyway. I never knew I once nearly didn't get a stocking. I don't remember a Christmas when there wasn't something in it. Mother said that when he came home and said: I've lost the stocking things, poor Barbie's stocking things: they set to and turned out drawers and cupboards looking for odds and ends for hours so as not to disappoint me and that I said it was the nicest stocking ever. But perhaps that's only how she remembered it. But it showed they loved me. I adored Christmas mornings. I always woke while it was still dark and worked my toes up and down to feel the stocking's weight and listen to the rustle and crackle. And then I'd sit up and sniff very cautiously to smell the magic, I mean of someone having been there who drove across frosty rooftops and had so many chimneys to attend to but never forgot mine.'

'Yes,' Mabel said. 'I remember that - the idea of a strange scene in the room, but I don't think I put the idea into words.'

'I don't suppose I did either. It's how I describe it now. As children we accept magic as a normal part of life. Everything was rooted in it, everything conspires in magic terms.' She laughed. 'Even the quarrels in our house had the darkness of magic in them, they were strange and incomprehensible and threatening as magic often is. I expected to find toads hopping on the staircase and misshapen things falling out of cupboards.'

'Poor Barbie.'

'No! My life was never dull.'

'Is it very dull now?'

'Now least of all.'

Paul Scott

ANNA KARENINA

Vronsky followed the guard to the carriage, and at the door of the compartment had to stop and make way for a lady who was getting out. His experience as a man of the world told him at a glance that she belonged to the best society. He begged her pardon and was about to enter the carriage but felt he must have another look at her - not because of her beauty, not on account of the elegance and unassuming grace of her whole figure, but because of something tender and caressing in her lovely face as she passed him. As he looked round, she too turned her head. Her brilliant grey eyes, shadowed by thick lashes, gave him a friendly, attentive look, as though she were recognizing him, and then turned to the approaching crowd as if in search of someone. In that brief glance Vronsky had time to notice the suppressed animation which played over her face and flitted between her sparkling eyes and the slight smile curving her red lips. It was as though her nature were so brimming over with something that against her will it expressed itself now in a radiant look, now in a smile. She deliberately shrouded the light in her eyes but in spite of herself it gleamed in the faintly perceptible smile.

Vronsky stepped into the carriage. His mother, a wizened old lady with black eyes and ringlets, screwed up her eyes to scan her son and her thin lips smiled slightly. Getting up from her seat and passing her bag to her maid, she extended her little wrinkled hand to her son to kiss; then, lifting his head from her hand, she kissed him on the cheek.

'You got my telegram? You are quite well? That's a mercy.'

'Did you have a good journey?' asked her son, sitting down beside her and involuntarily listening to a woman's voice outside the door. He knew it was the voice of the lady he had met as he entered the coach.

'All the same I do not agree with you,' said the lady's voice.

'That's the Petersburg way of looking at it, madame.'

'Not at all, simply a woman's way,' she replied.

'Well, well, allow me to kiss your hand.'

'Good-bye, Ivan Petrovich. And would you see if my brother is here and send him to me,' said the lady right at the door now and coming back into the compartment again.

'Well, have you found your brother?' asked Vronsky's mother, addressing the lady.

Vronsky realized now that this was Madame Karenin.

Leo Tolstoy

INDEX OF AUTHORS

INDEX OF TITLES

234

PUBLISHERS
of prose works from which
selections have been taken

GRADE FOUR:

The Fir Tree - *Hans Andersen* - several editions of Andersen's Fairy Tales
Jennings Goes To School - *Anthony Buckeridge* - MacMillan Children's Books
Moondial - *Helen Cresswell* - Puffin
The Mouse and His Child - *Russell Hoban* - New Windmill, Heinemann
The Tale of Jeremy Vole - *Stephen Lawhead* - Lion Publishing
The Story of King Arthur - *retold by Robin Lister* - Lion Publishing
The Revenge of Samuel Stokes - *Penelope Lively* - Mammoth
Five Children and It - *E Nesbit* - BBC Books

GRADE FIVE:

The Lion and The Mouse - *Aesop* - several editions of Aesop's Fables
Carrie's War - *Nina Bawden* - Hamish Hamilton
The Incredible Journey - *Sheila Burnford* - Hodder & Stoughton, Lythway
Large Print
Catweazle - *Richard Carpenter* - Puffin
The Animals Of Farthing Wood - *Colin Dann* - BBC Books
White Fang - *Jack London* - Penguin and other editions, sometimes in
collections
The Hobbit - *JRR Tolkien* - Allen & Unwin
The Birthday Of The Infanta - *Oscar Wilde* - several editions of his Children's
Stories or Fairy Stories, including Puffin *The Happy Prince And Other Stories*

GRADE SIX:

The Dark Is Rising - *Susan Cooper* - Bodley Head
The Never-Ending Story - *Michael Ende* - Penguin
Goggle-Eyes - *Anne Fine* - Hamish Hamilton, Puffin
Bambi's Children - *Felix Salten* - Souvenir Press
The Cricket In Times Square - *George Selden* - Puffin
Children On The Oregon Trail - *A Rutgers van der Loeff* - Puffin
Haphazard House - *Mary Wesley* - Sky Books, Longman
The Swiss Family Robinson - *Johann Wyss* - Everyman Library Children's
Classics

GRADE SEVEN:

My Uncle Silas - *H E Bates* - Penguin
George Silverman's Explanation - *Charles Dickens* - several editions, and any
Complete Works - often bound together with *Hard Times*
The Moon of Gomrath - *Alan Garner* - Harper Collins, Lion Books
Rice Without Rain - *Minfong Ho* - New Windmill, Heinemann Educational
To Kill a Mockingbird - *Harper Lee* - New Windmill
The Lake at the End of the World - *Caroline MacDonald* - Cascades, Collins

Ghost Song - *Susan Price* - Faber & Faber
I Capture the Castle - *Dodie Smith* - Red Fox

GRADE EIGHT:

Villette - *Charlotte Bronte* - many editions, including Penguin & Everyman
I'm the King of the Castle - *Susan Hill* - Heinemann, Penguin
Mr Norris Changes Trains - *Christopher Isherwood* - Methuen
The Tree of Hands - *Ruth Rendell* - Arrow Books
Wide Sargasso Sea - *Jean Rhys* - Bloomsbury Classics
Sons and Lovers - *D.H. Lawrence* - Penguin
Tono-Bungay - *H G Wells* - Everyman
Frost In May - *Antonia White* - Virago, New Windmill

BRONZE MEDAL:

The Way of Wyrd - *Brian Bates* - Beaver Books
A Particular Friendship - *Dirk Bogarde* - Penguin, Viking
The Moonstone - *Wilkie Collins* - OUP *(Three Great Novels)*
Daisy Miller - *Henry James* - Worlds Classics, OUP, Penguin
Miguel St - *V S Naipaul* - Caribbean Writers, Heinemann Educational, Penguin
A Far Cry From Kensington - *Muriel Spark* - Penguin
The Pearl - *John Steinbeck* - New Windmill, Heinemann Educational
Sir Harry Hotspur of Humblethwaite - *Anthony Trollope* - Pocket Classics,
    Sutton Publishers

SILVER MEDAL:

Sense and Sensibility - *Jane Austen* - Collins, etc
Cold Comfort Farm - *Stella Gibbons* - Penguin
Letters of Vincent Van Gogh - Flamingo
Brighton Rock - *Graham Greene* - Bodley Head, Penguin, Everyman,
    Heinemann
The Fall of the House of Usher - *Edgar Allan Poe* - Penguin
Off The Rails - *Lisa St Aubin de Teran* - Bloomsbury Press
The Age of Innocence - *Edith Wharton* - CUP, Everyman, Penguin
Spring Fever - *P G Wodehouse* - Penguin

GOLD MEDAL:

Clayhanger - *Arnold Bennett* - 20th Century Classics
Look At Me - *Anita Brookner* - Jonathan Cape, Penguin
Where Angels Fear To Tread - *E M Forster* - Penguin, 20th Century
    Classics etc
The Leopard - *Guiseppe Tomasi di Lampedusa* - Collins, Everyman
Titus Groan - *Mervyn Peake* - Mandarin
The Pigeon - *Patrick Süskind* - Penguin
The Secret History - *Donna Tartt* - Penguin
Decline and Fall - *Evelyn Waugh* - Everyman, 20th Century Classics etc

LLAM TEACHERS' DIPLOMA:

London Fields - *Martin Amis* - Penguin
The Life of Samuel Johnson - *James Boswell* - Penguin, Signet, Everyman etc
Wild Swans - *Jung Chang* - Flamingo
Bleak House - *Charles Dickens* - Collins, Everyman, Penguin etc
Foucault's Pendulum - *Umberto Eco* - Picador
A Grief Observed - *C S Lewis* - Faber & Faber
The Towers of Silence - *Paul Scott* - Penguin (part of *The Raj Quartet*)
Anna Karenina - *Leo Tolstoy* - Everyman, Penguin, OUP etc